Edited by Alan Durband

PLAYBILL TWO

Hutchinson Educational

HUTCHINSON EDUCATIONAL LTD
178–202 Great Portland Street, London W1

London Melbourne Sydney
Auckland Johannesburg Cape Town
and agencies throughout the world

First published 1969
Second impression 1970

Printed in Great Britain by litho on smooth wove paper
by Anchor Press, and bound by Wm. Brendon,
both of Tiptree, Essex

ISBN 0 09 105410 9 (c)
0 09 105411 7 (p)

Contents

Introduction

Playbill Two contains plays by David Shellan, Ann Jellicoe, David Perry, Tom Stoppard, and Stewart Conn.

1 The Plays

David Shellan's *Perfection City* and Ann Jellicoe's *The Rising Generation* are both seriously concerned about the problems of modern society. David Shellan's dramatic method is conventional comedy; Ann Jellicoe relies upon the immediacy of audience participation, theatre-in-the-round, and all the devices of avant-garde theatre.

Perfection City is a modern morality play. Its two principal characters, Homber and Deadbeat, appear at first to be a music-hall double-act, but as the play develops it is clear that they symbolise mankind, and have much in common with the tramps Vladimir and Estragon in Samuel Beckett's *Waiting for Godot*. Homber is the idealist, Deadbeat the common man. They live in an imperfect world, and though Deadbeat would be content with a few modest comforts (such as new boots and regular meals) he is prepared to be led by Homber, whose vision is greater and whose values are higher than his own.

Homber and Deadbeat encounter two typical obstructions to man's progress—symbolically represented by Cawaweekaw and Jackson. The semi-civilised Indian stands for those who live by alien and more warlike codes. The railroad boss represents Big Business, which puts material progress before ideals. At the end of the play the choice is between the world with all its imperfections and the world as it might be. For a moment Deadbeat is tempted to conform, persuaded by the worldly philosophy of Jackson, but Homber is indefatigable. Deadbeat is defeatist—to him Perfection City was 'a mighty good idea while it lasted'; but to Homber it is an attainable goal. Inspired by hope he is prepared to scale mountains in search of a valley where he can build Perfection.

Ann Jellicoe's *The Rising Generation* concentrates in one act the consequences that follow from mass prejudice in an age of inverted standards. Mother, a nature image normally associated with goodness, is projected in this play with nightmarish horror: she is savage and destructive, a perversion of the norm. At first she works upon the minds of the rabble and ultimately, in a desperate and destructive hatred, she uses her natural power in an obliterating nuclear explosion. Out of the fire comes the will to start anew, and once again man turns to the ship for a means of escape. With Noah it was the Ark. With the Pilgrim Fathers it was the *Mayflower*. With twentieth-century man it is a space-ship called *Hope*.

The third play in *Playbill Two*—David Perry's *As Good as New*—is a macabre comedy set in the suburban home of the Pimbles, who live in the shadow of imminent catastrophe. While Grandpa toils in the cellar on his corpses, the normal life of the family goes on from one fatality to the next— punctuated by Grandma's frequent trips to the WC to be sick, Mr Pimble's shattering cough, and June's siren wails of woe. The imperturbable Mrs Pimble's firm maternal management of affairs is the one rock-steady factor in this grotesque family situation. She has learned to compromise with fate, accepting the simple doctrine that it's never too late to mend.

The riddle of John Brown in Tom Stoppard's *A Separate Peace* (a television play adapted for this series) is so essentially simple that it baffles the hospital doctor and his staff. They naturally suspect things are more complicated than they turn out to be. A man who arrives at a nursing home in the early hours of the morning, carrying a case stuffed with pound notes and expecting the kind of service provided by an hotel, is bound to puzzle a profession that is geared exclusively to treating the sick. But John Brown says he isn't sick, and there is enough evidence in the text for us to agree that he isn't. Brown's vocation is 'to do nothing, and have nothing expected of him'; in worldly terms, abnormal enough to justify the doctor's careful observation of him. But Brown's philosophy has its own convincing logic, and we are left sharing his regret that, for him at least, it is a sad thing to be so well.

The last play in the volume is *Fancy Seeing You, Then* by Stewart Conn, a conversation piece that leads the eavesdropper up the garden path. Like Murray, we believe that Howatt's breezy flow of talk is based on a James Bond fantasy; we think he is trying to convince a provincial hick from Falkirk that he is big-time. Murray will never know what we, and the Waiter, know. The trick is done in a visual flash; a clever theatrical dénouement.

2 *The Playwrights*

David Shellan was born in 1931, and apart from National Service he has lived in the suburbs of London all his life. A journalist by profession, he has written some thirty plays since he first began to write in 1955. About half of them have been one-acters and several have won festival prizes. His full-length plays have had many amateur performances, including some at the Questor's Theatre, Ealing; one was given a professional production at the Comedy Theatre,

A*

London, in 1965. He is currently working on a commission for a thirty-minute play for BBC2.

Ann Jellicoe was born in 1927 and during her theatrical career has been an actress, a stage manager, and a director. She founded and ran the Cockpit Theatre Club to experiment with open-stage productions, and has taught at the Central School of Speech and Drama where she was once a pupil. In 1956 she won third prize in the *Observer* play competition with *The Sport of My Mad Mother*. Her next full-length play, *The Knack,* was produced in 1961 and later became an award-winning film. *The Rising Generation* was originally commissioned by the Girl Guides Association. They asked for a play 'of interest to youth', with 'a positive ending' and a cast of about 800 girls, 100 boys, and some adults. Failing to appreciate the brilliance of Miss Jellicoe's appeal to eye, ear and intellect, they rejected it. This is the play's first publication in book form.

David Perry was born in 1928. While at London University he was awarded a French Government scholarship in order to study drama at the Conservatoire de Paris, and later he spent eight years in various repertory companies as an actor. In 1964 he became director of Ipswich Arts Theatre, moving the following year to the Royal Academy of Dramatic Art, where he is now a lecturer. He has written five plays for TV and a full-length stage play. *As Good As New* is a revised and shortened version of his TV play *Stuff and Nonsense.*

Tom Stoppard was born in Czechoslovakia in 1937 and brought up in Singapore and India. He came to live in England in 1946, beginning his writing career as a journalist in Bristol, and turning freelance in 1960 when he began to write plays. His first was *A Walk on the Water,* televised in 1963 and produced on stage in Berlin and Vienna the following year. With some additions and a new title, *Enter a Free Man,* it was produced in London in 1968. During these years he wrote four radio plays and three TV plays, a novel *Lord Malquist and Mr Moon,* and his second and most famous play *Rosencrantz and Guildenstern are Dead.* This entered the repertoire of the National Theatre in 1967 and has since been performed in New York (winning the Critics and Tony awards), all over the Continent, and at theatres as far apart as Tokyo and Buenos Aires.

Stewart Conn was born in 1936. His most recent stage plays have been *I Didn't Always Live Here,* presented by Glasgow Citizens Theatre, and *The King,* which was performed at the Traverse Theatre during the 21st Edinburgh Festival. As well as writing for radio and television, Stewart Conn is an accomplished poet. His collection *Stoats in the Sunlight* was published by Hutchinson in 1968. He lives in Glasgow, a stone's throw from the BBC where he works as a radio drama producer.

Acknowledgements

For permission to publish the plays in this volume the editor is grateful to the following authors and their agents:
David Shellan and Messrs D. C. Benson and Campbell Thomson Ltd for *Perfection City*; David Perry and Messrs Film Rights Ltd for *As Good as New*; Ann Jellicoe and Miss Margaret Ramsay Ltd for *The Rising Generation*; Tom Stoppard and Fraser and Dunlop Ltd for *A Separate Peace*; Stewart Conn and Harvey Unna Ltd for *Fancy Seeing You, Then*.

No performance of these plays may be given unless a licence has been obtained. Applications should be addressed to the authors' agents.

Perfection City

DAVID SHELLAN

CAST

HOMBER
DEADBEAT
CAWAWEEKAW
JACKSON

Perfection City

SCENE: *The backcloth suggests a wide sweep of prairie with distant hills. On stage, to the right, a covered wagon whose frontier days are almost done. To the left, some scraps of vegetation suggesting a spring, near which sprawls* DEADBEAT, *his face covered entirely by an enormous hat. Beside him, the remains of a camp fire.* HOMBER *is pacing yards and calculating. Both are hobos and dress accordingly. Boxes, tins, pots and other rubbish are strewn across the stage. The lighting is brilliant white, suggesting heat. Towards the end of the play it mellows, suggesting dusk.*

HOMBER [*without looking round*]: Say, Deadbeat. [*No response. More sharply*] Deadbeat.

DEADBEAT [*moving hat sufficiently to uncover mouth*]: Yugh?

[*A monosyllable to strike despair to any heart less formidable than* HOMBER'*s*]

HOMBER: The city hall'll be right here.

DEADBEAT: Say, Homber, when do we eat?

HOMBER: Between the library and the concert hall.

DEADBEAT: Culture gives me indigestion.

HOMBER: This'll be the city centre. Gee, it makes me feel kinda warm inside.

DEADBEAT [*scratching himself*]: Ya like horsemeat?

HOMBER: Sure I like horsemeat.

DEADBEAT: That was the last horse we had back at the border where I got these goddam itches. Ya like prairie dog?

HOMBER: Ain't particular.

DEADBEAT [*lifting object vaguely resembling a rat*]: That's what we got. Cooked or cold?

HOMBER: Guess I ain't all that hungry.

DEADBEAT: Guess I ain't too.

[*Pause*]

Say, how far d'ya think it is to Frisco?

HOMBER: Frisco? That's a sinful town.

DEADBEAT [*delighted*]: Yugh. Sure is sinful.

HOMBER: We ain't gonna go to Frisco.

DEADBEAT: Gotta go some place.

HOMBER: We're stopping right here.

DEADBEAT: I can't wait to get to Frisco.

HOMBER: I said we're stopping right here.

DEADBEAT: They got dames in Frisco.

HOMBER: Deadbeat, we're stopping right here.

DEADBEAT: They call 'em Frisco friskies. Shucks, they're some sheilas.

HOMBER [*exasperated, shaking him*]: Here, ya wacky-eared moron, right here.

DEADBEAT: Don't shake me, ya lousy mixed-up Republican.

HOMBER: Well I'm trying to tell ya and all ya do is talk about sin.

DEADBEAT: Say, you got something better to talk about?

HOMBER: Sure have. Perfection, Deadbeat. This is it. We're stopping right here.

DEADBEAT [*surveying auditorium*]: Perfection? Guess I'm kinda short-sighted.

HOMBER: In the middle of the great prairie right under God's own sun.

DEADBEAT [*settling down again*]: Happy noo year.

HOMBER [*indicating the spring*]: There's water.

DEADBEAT: Way down.

HOMBER: And virgin earth.

DEADBEAT: Nothing could be virginer.

HOMBER [*ecstatic*]: So this is where our city shall be. Perfection City, United States of America.

DEADBEAT [*scratching*]: Stop it, Homber. You're making me uncomfortable.

[HOMBER *brings from the wagon a crudely made board reading, in indifferent lettering, 'Welcome to Perfection'*]

DEADBEAT [*getting up, alarmed*]: Homber, ya're not serious?

HOMBER: Sure am.

DEADBEAT: What, here?

HOMBER: Right here.

DEADBEAT: In the middle of a goddam desert?

HOMBER: How many times have I told ya? Ya gotta have vision.

DEADBEAT [*looking round again*]: Yugh. Sure have.

HOMBER: I'm telling ya, fifty years from now this city will be heaven on earth.

DEADBEAT: Yugh. And look what happened to Heaven-on-Earth, Nebraska. That was going fine for just a coupla days.

HOMBER: The ideal wasn't wrong, Deadbeat.

DEADBEAT: No, the land just didn't happen to be ours. Know what they're building there now? The State pen.

HOMBER: That's a place won't be needed in Perfection. We're gonna have a library instead.

DEADBEAT: Ya gonna lock up drunks in a library?

HOMBER: There ain't gonna be no drunks.

DEADBEAT: No drunks? What'll the marshal do?

HOMBER: We ain't gonna need no marshal.

DEADBEAT: No marshal? Shucks, every goddam hobo in the country'll be here tomorrow.

HOMBER: Ya see, Perfection is gonna be a city where there's nothing but love. Every single critter loves every other critter and there ain't no hard words spoken. So what's the use of a marshal?

DEADBEAT: How about keeping the Injuns off?

HOMBER: There ain't gonna be no Injun-fighting in Perfection.

DEADBEAT: You say so?

HOMBER: The constitootion says so.

DEADBEAT: Aw shucks, we got one of them?

HOMBER: It's the very first thing we gotta have.

DEADBEAT: The Injuns gonna read it?

HOMBER: Sure they're gonna read it. The Injuns'll belong to Perfection. Perfection belongs to every critter. God loves every goddam hobo.

DEADBEAT: Injun city, ugh?

HOMBER: Injun and hobo, hobo and Injun. Brudders under the prairie sky. Ain't that wonderful?

DEADBEAT [*ironic*]: Yugh, that's wonderful.

HOMBER: Every critter'll have equal rights.

DEADBEAT: Have what?

HOMBER: Equal rights.

DEADBEAT: Where d'ya pick that up?

HOMBER: Ya never heard of Jefferson?

DEADBEAT [*looking ruefully at his bare feet*]: Was he the skunk pinched ma boots back in Indiana?

HOMBER: No critter pinched ya boots. They fell off. I keep telling ya. Jefferson was the greatest critter ever lived.

DEADBEAT: Then he ought to have got boots of his own.

HOMBER: He'd got boots of his own. Will ya shut up about

boots? I don't wanna hear about boots. Your boots fell off in Indiana and that's the end.

[*Pause*]

DEADBEAT: Say, Homber.

HOMBER [*who is bringing out junk from the wagon*]: Yugh?

DEADBEAT: This equal rights.

HOMBER: Yugh?

DEADBEAT: Does it include boots?

HOMBER: Sure it includes boots.

DEADBEAT: You got boots.

HOMBER: Sure I got boots. I live good.

DEADBEAT: I'm the only critter ain't got boots. Jefferson's gotta down on me.

HOMBER: Jefferson wasn't worried about boots. He worried about other things.

DEADBEAT: What did he worry about?

HOMBER: The constitootion.

DEADBEAT [*dejected*]: I wanna go Frisco.

HOMBER: Listen. This critter Jefferson wrote the Declaration of Independence.

DEADBEAT [*impressed*]: He could write?

HOMBER: Sure he could write. He was president.

DEADBEAT: Could he read as well?

HOMBER: Sure he could read.

DEADBEAT: I feel kinda stoopid. I can't go on.

HOMBER: It's just because of Jefferson **ya can** go on, ya lousy son of a bitch. All critters are created equal. That's what he said.

DEADBEAT: Did he say that?

HOMBER: Sure did. Wrote it down. All critters are created equal.

DEADBEAT: But you've got boots and I ain't.

HOMBER [*exasperated*]: I got boots because I tie them on. That's why I got boots. Now come and help me build Perfection.

DEADBEAT: We gonna build it now?

HOMBER: Sure. No sense wasting time. [*Handing him a pile of wood*] Here, catch hold of this.

DEADBEAT: What is it?

HOMBER: It's the city hall.

DEADBEAT [*after an uncomprehending pause*]: The what?

HOMBER: The city hall. The roof. [*Handing him another pile*] This is the floor. You can start.

DEADBEAT: I can start. I can start?

HOMBER: Building. Ya can start building.

DEADBEAT [*gazing into the distance*]: Where can I start building?

HOMBER [*pointing to his feet*]: Right there, clophead.

DEADBEAT: The city hall. Right here.

HOMBER: Right there.

[*Pause while* DEADBEAT *drops wood at his feet and examines it*]

DEADBEAT: Say, what goes in the city hall?

HOMBER: The big shots. Critters who run the place.

DEADBEAT: We gonna have big shots?

HOMBER: Gotta have someone to organise.

DEADBEAT: Who they gonna be?

HOMBER: Well, guess we gotta have a president to start with.

DEADBEAT: What's he do?

HOMBER: He signs the constitootion.

DEADBEAT: I can't write.

HOMBER: Then I declare myself elected.

DEADBEAT: You?

HOMBER: By a landslide.

DEADBEAT: Since when could you write?

HOMBER: We gotta have schools. This ignorance is goddam appalling. We gotta teach these hobos. I wanna sign the constitootion right now.

[*Deadbeat begins to look for the constitution*]

Deadbeat, the constitootion ain't written yet.

DEADBEAT: That so? Well, you go right ahead and write it.

HOMBER: I can't. It ain't constitootional. The president signs it. Some other critter's gotta write it.

DEADBEAT: There ain't no other critter.

HOMBER: There's you, ya moron.

DEADBEAT: Now listen to me, I'm no moron. Besides, I can't write.

HOMBER: You gotta start learning. You're the noo saccertaria state.

DEADBEAT: The noo what?

HOMBER: Saccertaria state.

DEADBEAT: Who says so?

HOMBER: I say so.

DEADBEAT: I ain't been elected.

HOMBER: Ya don't have to be elected. I appoint you.

DEADBEAT: Ya do?

HOMBER: Because I'm president. [*As* DEADBEAT *sits again*] What are ya squatting for now?

DEADBEAT [*scratching*]: I'm thinking.

HOMBER: We ain't got time—

DEADBEAT: I don't give a bellyache about the time. Things are happening to me. I gotta think, else I'll grow up ignorant. And my big toe hurts.

[*An arrow appears in the 'Welcome' board*]

HOMBER: What was that?

DEADBEAT: Yugh, must have been.

HOMBER: Sounded like—

DEADBEAT: Yugh, that's what I figured.

HOMBER: Goes to show how deceptive sounds can be.

DEADBEAT: Sure does.

HOMBER: Ya just can't trust no sound no place.

DEADBEAT: I'd never trust no sound nowise myself.

[*They see, and react to, the arrow simultaneously*]

Say, Homber.

HOMBER: Yugh?

DEADBEAT: D'ya suppose this has any significance?

HOMBER: Yugh. Guess it does.

DEADBEAT: What d'ya suppose it signifies?

HOMBER: Injuns.

DEADBEAT: I kinda thought that's what you'd say.

HOMBER: It's the Injun's way of commoonicating.

DEADBEAT [*backing slowly*]: Injun and hobo, hobo and Injun, just wrapped up together, ya said?

HOMBER: Sure. Just perfect love.

DEADBEAT: Homber.

HOMBER: Yugh?

DEADBEAT: Frisco's this way.

HOMBER: We ain't gonna go to Frisco.

DEADBEAT: I just feel kinda lonesome.

HOMBER: We're not quitting now, yallerback.

DEADBEAT: I just feel kinda attached to my scalp.

> [DEADBEAT *has now reached the wings where*
> CAWAWEEKAW, *a tall brave with bare torso, is standing*
> *motionless behind him. As* DEADBEAT *slowly backs into him,*
> *he is gagged and his hands tied with wholly theatrical*
> *rapidity*]

HOMBER [*unaware*]: The Injuns are my constitooents, Deadbeat. If they wanna commoonicate they can go right ahead.

CAWAWEEKAW: Brother, I speak peace.

HOMBER: Ugh?

CAWAWEEKAW: I speak peace.

HOMBER [*delighted*]: He speaks American. Our first vote.

CAWAWEEKAW: Learn lingo from former scalps.

HOMBER [*checked*]: Of course, we don't know which way.

CAWAWEEKAW: Speak American extremely well. Goddam
critter and lousy son of a bitch.

HOMBER: Say, you've been listening.

CAWAWEEKAW: Name, Cawaweekaw.

HOMBER: Come again?

CAWAWEEKAW: Cawaweekaw.

HOMBER: That's quite an achievement. Would you mind

very much letting go the lousy lump of horsemeat ya got there?

CAWAWEEKAW [*indicating Deadbeat*]: This?

HOMBER: Yugh, that. I guess it's not much but it's kinda all I got.

[DEADBEAT, *released, runs towards* HOMBER *but is jerked back by the rope held by* CAWAWEEKAW. HOMBER *pulls gag from mouth*]

DEADBEAT [*howling*]: Homber, scratch me urgently.

HOMBER [*doing so*]: I keep telling ya, ya should look where ya sit.

DEADBEAT: It don't matter where I sit. They kinda travel with me.

HOMBER: Listen. We'll give this naked critter an interview. You're the interpreter.

DEADBEAT: The what?

HOMBER: All ya gotta do is tell me what the critter says.

DEADBEAT: But he speaks the lingo—he said so.

HOMBER: It ain't dignified for a president to speak direct. Tell him he's welcome to Perfection, the city of brotherly love.

DEADBEAT [*to Cawaweekaw*]: You're sure welcome to it.

CAWAWEEKAW: Land here—tribe's.

HOMBER: Well, go on, Deadbeat—interpret.

DEADBEAT [*adding elaborate gestures*]: Land here, tribe's.

HOMBER: Tell him the president ain't fixed the city boundary yet.

DEADBEAT: No city boundary.

CAWAWEEKAW: No city.

DEADBEAT: Says there's no city. Pretty fast thinker.

HOMBER: Tell him the city'll be here in a day or two.

DEADBEAT: City here pretty soon.

CAWAWEEKAW: Beg to differ, et cetera.

HOMBER [*delighted*]: Ya see? He's had a business education.

CAWAWEEKAW [*suddenly communicative*]: Dear sir, extremely interested in bizniz. Listen, will tell. White man once come to red man's camp. Fur-lined boots. Beeeg bizniz.

HOMBER: What became of him?

CAWAWEEKAW: Use scalp as typewriter cover.

HOMBER: Business men never stay one place long. Like me and Deadbeat, till today. Now we're gonna go no place. We're stopping right here.

CAWAWEEKAW: You say?

HOMBER: Sure I say. We're gonna build Perfection. It's all in the wagon.

CAWAWEEKAW: You have wagon full of perfection?

DEADBEAT: It's fulla rotten wood.

HOMBER: Deadbeat, where's ya vision?

DEADBEAT: That's where I got these goddam itches, from that lousy hunk.

HOMBER: Ya gotta have vision to build Perfection. Ya gotta see it clean and clear like a blue sky. Gotta see it as it will be. A place we can live in like buddies, way out here on the prairie. Ya gotta admit, it's a great ideal.

CAWAWEEKAW [*sharpening hatchet on what looks like a strop fixed to a belt*]: Most great.

HOMBER: You think Jefferson be proud of me?

CAWAWEEKAW: You say?

HOMBER: Jefferson. Greatest critter ever lived.

CAWAWEEKAW: Regret not officially informed.

HOMBER: We sure need schools in Perfection. Say, I gotten idea.

DEADBEAT: Aw, shucks, no.

HOMBER: Say we start Perfection with a big celebration? Get all the folk in the city centre with a big bonfire and a big dance? Say, can you dance, Deadbeat?

DEADBEAT [*indignant*]: Ma boots were pinched in Indiana.

HOMBER: What's the matter with the bare feet God gave ya?

DEADBEAT: The big toe hurts.

CAWAWEEKAW: Me dance extremely well.

HOMBER: That so?

CAWAWEEKAW: See. [*He does a few steps*]

HOMBER: Guess that's good. How about that, Deadbeat?

DEADBEAT: It ain't commercial.

: And no swearing. Make that the next goddam law.

: Just you show ya cringing copper-hoofed yaller
a deadalive Injun. [*Fires into the air*] Just you wait
feel the noo machine gun. It'll chop ya legs off
of a minute.

Critters will love each other. That's law number

: What's this then? Two-legged movables laced up?
ion? Gee, these salesmen don't waste much time.

Glad to know ya. My name's Homber.

: Hi. Who's ya friend?

That's Deadbeat.

That ain't a name, it's a description. I'm John
a Jackson.

: Homber—he must be the skunk pinched my

Little man, did I hear you say skunk?

: B-b-back in Indiana.

I ain't been to Indiana for years. Not since the
came out west. That's my job, the railroad. Been
Injuns all day. What did you say your name was?

'm Homber. I'm the president.

Yugh? What of?

This city.

What city?

HOMBER: It'll do fine. We gotta have originality. D'ya know
any other Injuns with party pieces?

CAWAWEEKAW: Tribe have interesting and absorbing hobby.
Collect war dances.

HOMBER: Say, that's wonderful. We'll call them peace dances.
We'll have the city centre here—just an open space with
flowers and fountains and cute little statues, like in Liquor
Town, Ohio. And the Injuns can come on to the square
and do their peace dance.

CAWAWEEKAW: See, will demonstrate. [*He capers round the
'Welcome' board*]

HOMBER: Say, can we join in?

CAWAWEEKAW: Follow me.

HOMBER: Whoopee.

[*As they scamper round,* CAWAWEEKAW *seizes the rope and
pulls in* DEADBEAT, *whose hands no-one has remembered to
untie. He quickly involves* HOMBER *in the tangle and ties
both of them to the board.* HOMBER *faces away from*
CAWAWEEKAW]

Say, that dance is sure something. That dance'd sure be a
hit back in Boston. Is this how it ends?

CAWAWEEKAW: Always.

HOMBER: Kinda captivating, Deadbeat, ugh?

DEADBEAT: I'd rather not think too much just now, Homber,
d'ya mind.

HOMBER: What happens now?

CAWAWEEKAW: Braves dance round.

HOMBER: Say, we'll have a ringside seat.

CAWAWEEKAW [*again sharpening hatchet*]: Other braves make preparations.

DEADBEAT: Homber.

HOMBER: Yugh?

DEADBEAT: Guess it's too late to go to Frisco.

HOMBER: That's it, we're stopping right here.

DEADBEAT: That's the way I feel.

HOMBER: Perfection's gonna be just lovely, Deadbeat, I can see it now.

DEADBEAT: What I can see ain't so lovely.

HOMBER: You gotta have vision, I keep telling ya.

DEADBEAT: I got vision all right.

HOMBER: We've been looking for Perfection for a mighty long time, me and you, Deadbeat. Been right across this land of promise but it's been worth getting here.

DEADBEAT: Then you'll die happy, Homber.

HOMBER: Shucks, I ain't begun living yet. Perfection's made me a noo man. Say, what's the Injun doing now? Is it all over?

DEADBEAT: Yugh, very soon.

HOMBER: Is he gonna cut us loose?

DEADBEAT: Yugh, that's right. Gonna cut us loose.

[*But* CAWAWEEKAW'S *advance gunshots*]

CAWAWEEKAW [*drawing back*]:

HOMBER: Do I hear shooting?

CAWAWEEKAW: Regret must w

HOMBER: Shooting's not permi

CAWAWEEKAW: Regret unable

HOMBER: Say, you're not goin

[*More shots*]

CAWAWEEKAW: Reluctantly c

HOMBER: Drop in any time.

CAWAWEEKAW: You too kin favours, yours faithfully.

[*More shots. Exit* CAWAWEE

HOMBER: Say, Deadbeat, wh tootion put in something a

[*More shots*]

There's gonna be no noise

DEADBEAT: No noise.

HOMBER: Nothing but beau

.[*Enter* JOHN JEFFERSON JA ammunition belts. *Two revo*

JACKSON [*shouting*]: Come bitch, I wanna fill ya full

HOMBER

JACKSO face, till ya inside

HOMBER three.

JACKSO Perfec

HOMBER

JACKSON

HOMBER

JACKSON Jefferso

DEADBEA boots.

JACKSON

DEADBEA

JACKSON railroac chasing

HOMBER:

JACKSON

HOMBER:

JACKSON

HOMBER: The city we're gonna build here. Perfection.

JACKSON: You gonna build it?

HOMBER: Me and Deadbeat.

JACKSON: Yugh?

HOMBER: Wanna help?

JACKSON: I tell ya, I'm on the railroad.

HOMBER: Me and Deadbeat, then.

JACKSON [*having cut them loose by now*]: Listen, fella. I ain't got time to play games. There ain't gonna be no city here.

HOMBER: Who says so?

JACKSON: Railroad boss, that's who says so. Railroad boss says where the cities go. If ya don't wanna job with the railroad, ya gotta clear off out. Okay?

HOMBER: I ain't moving. I'm building Perfection right here.

DEADBEAT: Say, steady, Homber. The guy's offering us a job.

JACKSON: You used to work?

DEADBEAT: We've had our disagreements.

JACKSON: On this job ya live rough and work hard.

DEADBEAT: Any dough?

JACKSON: A kinda rumour.

DEADBEAT: Any chance getting to Frisco?

JACKSON: If ya don't get mislaid by Injuns.

DEADBEAT: That figures.

JACKSON: Like the one nearly had ya then. We're gonna build a fort here, so the railroad comes right through.

HOMBER: A fort? Here in Perfection?

JACKSON: To fight the Injuns.

HOMBER: You're gonna fight them?

JACKSON: Only way to stop them fighting us. Listen, son, I like ya. I'm giving ya the chance to go dream some place else. Mighty soon we're gonna rip through those belly-aching yallerbacks like a knife in the guts. We gotta noo kinda machine gun—wait till ya hear—

HOMBER [*turning away in pain*]: I don't wanna hear.

JACKSON [*bewildered*]: But I tell ya, it's scientific.

HOMBER: I don't wanna hear. We're building our city right where you're standing and there ain't gonna be no guns at all.

JACKSON: Be sensible, will ya—

HOMBER: We're gonna build Perfection in this place and in no other.

JACKSON: Brudder, that sure is rash talking. [JACKSON *crosses to* DEADBEAT *and rolls a wad of notes in front of him*] Say, fella, remember how to eat?

DEADBEAT: The memory ain't so good.

JACKSON: You and ya baxy buddy gotta go and quick.

DEADBEAT: Gotta go?

JACKSON [*handling gun*]: That's what I said.

DEADBEAT: I ain't disputing.

JACKSON: Take a few of these. It's called dough.

DEADBEAT: Yugh, I remember.

JACKSON: Enough for a square feed. D'ya want boots as well?

DEADBEAT: It'd be kinda convenient.

JACKSON: Get a job with the railroad.

DEADBEAT: Where?

JACKSON [*pointing right*]: Way back.

DEADBEAT [*pointing left*]: What's that way?

JACKSON: The mountains. Injuns. No food. No place to handle dough. Plenty of space for two corpses. If ya're not outa here in five minutes, you'll be getting in the way.

DEADBEAT: So ya said.

JACKSON: I'll be back. If you're not as baxy as your friend I'll see ya later on the railroad—that way. [*He makes to go off right, but hesitates and turns to* HOMBER *as if impelled to explain*] Listen, fella. Mebbe what we do ain't right but who's the hobo knows right from wrong? If we don't kill the Injuns, they kill us. Your skin or mine—and brudder, there's no choice in that. [*A parting shot to* DEADBEAT] Five minutes, critter.

[*Exit* JACKSON. *There is a pause while* DEADBEAT *packs their garbage into the wagon. Lights dim slightly to suggest a sinking sun*]

DEADBEAT [*gently*]: Homber. Gotta move, ya lousy old coyote. Gotta saddle up and jog on over. [*Pause*] You still sore? It was a mighty good idea while it lasted. So what?

It lays itself down and dies, just like every other goddam thing on this stinking earth. [*Pause*] Guess there'll be jobs for both of us on the railroad, Homber. That's food and sleep kinda regular. Guess I might get boots. That's kinda something. Might even be noo ones.

HOMBER [*who has been motionless, gazing leftwards*]: Say, Deadbeat.

DEADBEAT: Yugh?

HOMBER: What d'ya see way over there?

DEADBEAT: Just mountains.

HOMBER: What's it like in the mountains?

DEADBEAT: Cold, I guess.

HOMBER: Yugh. Cold and kinda clean.

DEADBEAT: Well, guess we're all set. Coming, Homber?

HOMBER: Say, Deadbeat, in those mountains there'd be water. And good soil, mebbe, virgin earth. Right up there in the mountains there'd be a place for Perfection, Deadbeat, some little valley, right away from everything, some little place to build our city. [*He takes over the wagon and pulls it to the left*]

DEADBEAT: But, Homber, listen—

HOMBER: Whatya waiting for, clophead? We gotta go build Perfection in the mountains.

DEADBEAT [*looking right*]: But the railroad—food and sleep—

HOMBER: Ya gotta choose, Deadbeat.

DEADBEAT: Homber, listen, gimme time to think.

HOMBER: I ain't got time to wait. Perfection's not the waiting sort of city. Are ya coming?

DEADBEAT [*torn between the two sides of the stage*]: It's just that I'd kinda like to have boots.

HOMBER [*starting off*]: So long, Deadbeat.

DEADBEAT [*a cry*]: Homber, don't leave me.

HOMBER [*stopping*]: You gonna come?

DEADBEAT: Guess I gotta have something more than just boots.

HOMBER [*delighted*]: You gonna help me build Perfection?

DEADBEAT [*with him now at the wagon*]: I guess we can build Perfection any goddam place—if anyone'll let us.

[*They move off*]

THE END

The Rising Generation

ANN JELLICOE

CAST

CHARLADIES	ERRAND BOY
OLD WOMEN	JOAN
MOTHER	STEPHEN
TEACHER	GIRLS AND BOYS

VOICE OVER LOUDSPEAKER

SCIENTIST

MARSHALS

The audience too may be encouraged to take part in the action

The Rising Generation

SCENE: *House lights up. Stage lights up. The audience,
assembled and seated, becomes aware of shouts and cries and
the sound of buckets being banged. The noise comes from a
crew of obstreperous* CHARLADIES. *The* CHARLADIES *carry
mops and buckets. They are dressed as old or oldish women
and may wear half-masks which make them look evil and
mischievous. The* CHARLADIES *are all over the auditorium.
They pass along the front rows of the various arena blocks
collecting refuse.*

CHARLADIES [*confused cries, not in unison*]: Orange peel, sweet
papers, ice cream cartons, tea cups, cigarette ends, don't
drop them on the floor, pick 'em up, pick 'em up, pass them
along please, keep Britain tidy, etc., etc., *ad lib.*

[*Another platoon of* CHARLADIES *is sweeping the arena
systematically in groups, like the men who brush the surface of
the ice during an ice show. The movement begins to be so
formal as to be a ritual dance.
The house lights now begin to fade*]

CHARLADIES [*sweeping the arena and speaking in unison.
Two-two time*]: Right! [*Pause*] Yes! [*Pause*] Right! [*Pause*]
Right! [*Pause*]
And round we go!
Right! [*Pause*] Yes! [*Pause*] Right! [*Pause*]
And round we go!

Right! Two! Three! Four!
And round we go!
Right, left, right, left, right, left, right, left
Right, left, right, left, right, left, right, left
And round we go!

[*They now march and countermarch with their mops over
their shoulders, their feet stamping out the rhythm. At the
finish, each* CHARLADY *faces outward towards a section of the
audience.
Sound of a penny whistle being played off. Enter an*
ERRAND BOY *on a bicycle, gay and cheeky. He steers the
bicycle with one hand and holds the whistle to his mouth
with the other. He weaves around the arena. (If the stage is
confined, he could be a boy selling newspapers.)
The* CHARLADIES *are evidently annoyed and shout angrily*]

CHARLADIES: Here! Clear off, you! No men! Get out, man!
Man, go home! We don't like your sort here, etc., etc., *ad
lib.*

[*A few of the* CHARLADIES *chase him with their mops.
Exit* ERRAND BOY, *still gay and cheeky.
Drum Roll. Music for* 'God Save the Queen'. *The
audience will, of course, rise and every encouragement should
be given to them to sing. The* CHARLADIES *amongst the
audience sing.
There is also massed singing over the loudspeakers*]

LOUDSPEAKER [*at the end of the verse, before the audience has
time to sit*] : You can sing louder than that.

CHARLADIES [*to each other and to the audience*]: You can sing
louder than that! They can sing louder than that, can't they!
Yes, they can! Let's have it again! Come on, you sing
much louder than that.

LOUDSPEAKER: Let's have it again, and this time let's raise the roof. Give 'em the words.

[*Drum roll. Words lowered on sheet.* 'God Save the Queen' *repeated. At the end of the verse, drum roll*]

LOUDSPEAKER [*above the drum roll*]: Here comes mother! Mother! Make way for mother!

[*All the* CHARLADIES *in the arena and in the audience take up the cry*]

CHARLADIES: Mother! Mother! Mother! Mother!

[*Drum roll continues.*
Enter MOTHER. MOTHER *is an enormous woman half-masked with padded head-dress and shoes. She is seated on top of a large ascending ladder of the type used for repairing overhead lights—that is, a ladder travelling on its own truck. The ladder is gaily decked out and is drawn by* OLD WOMEN *wearing half-masks, some of them harnessed to the truck.* MOTHER *holds reins and she also has a whip which she cracks around her. She is accompanied by a vast procession of* GIRLS *with half-masks representing* OLD WOMEN, *some carrying banners with slogans such as 'I hate men'; 'Men go home'; Dirty men'; etc., etc. Some carry portraits of* MOTHER. *Some clap hands in rhythm, some bang dust-bin lids*]

ALL: I hate men! Down with men! I hate men! Down with men! I hate men! Down with men! etc., etc.

[MOTHER *reaches the centre of the arena. She rises. Standing on top of the travelling ladder. Silence. The following speech is punctuated with cheers*]

MOTHER: This day I proclaim the Republic of Women! The Republic of Women! I proclaim the Republic of Women!

The Nation of Women! The Commonwealth of Women!
The World of Women! [*Long and loud cheers*] I hate niggers!
I hate Jews! I hate wogs! But most of all—I hate men!
[*Cheers*] Let us destroy men. Let us rid the world of men.
Let us make the world safe for women! Kill! Maim! Burn!
And if any women who love men remain—and if any man
or woman who is for men and against me—then the final
weapon! The irrevocable! The bomb! I shall not hesitate
to use the strength given to me! In defence. [*Cheers*]
I shall eat—

ALL [*softly*]: Men!

MOTHER: I shall drink—

ALL: Men!

MOTHER: I shall destroy—

ALL: Men!

MOTHER: Destroy—

ALL: Men!

MOTHER: Destroy—

ALL: Men!

MOTHER: Destroy—

ALL: Men!

[*This chant rises to a climax. At the height, everybody gives a
great screaming cry.* BLACKOUT. *Noise continues. Machine-
gun fire. A sound of running feet and cries in the arena and all
round the passages. Lights begin to swivel across the stage like
searchlights, to show women running in all directions.
Sometimes a man runs across and machine-gun fire is renewed.*

BLACKOUT. *Machine-gun fire.* LIGHTS UP.
A Rough Tribunal. The 'Judge' is MOTHER *on a rostrum, and
there is a rabble around her much like the tricoteuses at the
guillotine*]

MOTHER [*banging gavel, full of excitement*]: The accused! The
accused!

RABBLE [*confused roar*]: The accused, bring him up, etc., *ad lib.*

[*A* MAN *is dragged forward*]

MOTHER: What's the accusation?

1ST CHARLADY: It's a man, a man.

RABBLE: A man, a man.

MOTHER: Guilty or not guilty?

RABBLE: Guilty, guilty.

MOTHER: Guilty.

[*She bangs her gavel. A great yell.* MAN *is torn to bits.
Machine-gun fire. Lights fade. Lights up to show* MOTHER,
this time as an auctioneer, and a MAN *standing beside her*]

MOTHER [*with intense energy and excitement*]: A man for sale.
I'm selling a man! Lot 44. [*Roars of delight*] What am I bid?
What am I bid? A fine specimen of a man. You don't see
them much nowadays. Shall we say five pounds? [*Groans*]
Not five pounds? Too much at five pounds? All right, then.
Who'll give me a bid, who'll start me off? Come on, ladies,
a fine figure of a man, you don't often see a real man
nowadays. More likely in the Natural History Museum.
Stuffed.

VOICE: Give you half a dollar.

[VOICES *now become sharp, excited, lusting.* MAN *starts to be pushed around and gradually the movement becomes bigger so that he is pushed from one group to another, the movement getting larger and larger*]

MOTHER: Half-a-crown, half-a-crown.

2ND VOICE: Three bob.

MOTHER: Three bob, three bob.

3RD VOICE: Three-and-six.

MOTHER: Three-and-six, three-and-six.

4TH VOICE: Four shillings.

5TH VOICE: Four-and-six.

6TH VOICE: Five shillings.

7TH VOICE: Five shillings.

8TH VOICE: Five shillings.

9TH VOICE: Five-and-six.

10TH VOICE: Six shillings.

11TH VOICE: Six bob.

12TH VOICE: Six bob.

MOTHER: Six bob.

GROUP ONE: Six bob, six bob.

1ST VOICE: Six bob.

GROUP TWO: Six bob.

2ND VOICE: Six bob.

ALL: Six bob, six bob, six bob.

MOTHER: Six bob, that's what a man's worth. Six bob. Going! Going!

[*She points her gavel. The* MAN *is in the centre, untouched, bemused, the* WOMEN *all around him.*
Pause.
Enter JOAN, *a young girl, unmasked, dressed in white. She stands in a spotlight of bright pink.* JOAN *screams. Her voice diverts for an instant the attention of the* OLD WOMEN. *The* MAN *seizes his opportunity and darts away. They follow him like a swarm of bees. Eventually he escapes through one of the exits behind* JOAN. *The* WOMEN *seethe around her and run after him, so that the effect is of water rushing past her.*
Exit MAN *and rabble of* WOMEN.
JOAN *now begins to move gently in the spotlight. Music starts. Her movements grow into a dance which is confined to the spotlight. The dance should express the thoughts and emotions of a young girl, and it is confined to the spot in order to make this lighted area into a 'special place'.*
Machine-gun fire. JOAN *stops dancing.*
Enter STEPHEN. STEPHEN *is a boy of about eighteen. He is pursued by spotlights which try to find and hold him just as searchlights do an aeroplane. As soon as one light catches him, two or three others join the first. A sound of pounding feet and cries off. It is a small group of* WOMEN *dashing through the passages of the arena before they come on. Enter small group of* WOMEN]

1ST WOMAN: There he is.

[GENERAL CRY. *They run for* STEPHEN. JOAN *darts forward, grabs* STEPHEN *and takes him back to the pink spotlight.*

The small group of WOMEN *runs straight on and out.
Eventually the machine-gun fire fades out and lights go out,
with the exception.of the light on* JOAN *and* STEPHEN.
Pause]

STEPHEN: I'm Steve.

JOAN: Steve.

STEPHEN: What's your name?

[JOAN *laughs*]

STEPHEN: What's your name?

[JOAN *laughs and darts away.* STEPHEN *follows her. In one
section of the arena, small spotlights shine directly down. In
between these spotlights they chase each other, laughing
gently. Eventually* STEPHEN *catches* JOAN]

JOAN: Joan.

STEPHEN: Joan.

[*They start to dance together among the spotlights. A school-
bell ringing off. Enter an old masked* WOMAN, *who is the
teacher, at the head of a 'crocodile' of* GIRLS *all dressed in white.
Their hair is scraped back and they all wear enormous pairs of
spectacles. They carry exercise books from which they read as
they march. When they hear the bell—*]

GIRLS: Shakespeare was a woman.

TEACHER: Milton was a woman.

GIRLS: Milton was a woman.

TEACHER: The Black Prince was a woman.

GIRLS: The Black Prince was a woman.

TEACHER: Robin Hood, she was a woman.

GIRLS: Robin Hood, she was a woman.

TEACHER: King John was a woman.

GIRLS: King John was a woman.

TEACHER: Isaac Newton was a woman.

GIRLS: Isaac Newton was a woman.

[*Enter* GIRL, *also dressed in white, but her hair is loose and she wears no spectacles. She has been trying to catch the others up and is breathless with running*]

TEACHER: Girl!

GIRL: Yes, miss?

TEACHER: Your hair! Your spectacles, where are they?

GIRL: I'm sorry, miss.

TEACHER: Put your hair up, it's disgusting.

[*The* GIRL *takes spectacles from her pocket and puts them on and ties her hair up*]

TEACHER [*turning back to class*]: Shakespeare?

GIRLS: Woman!

TEACHER: Milton?

GIRLS: Woman!

TEACHER: Black Prince?

GIRLS: Woman!

TEACHER: Robin Hood?

GIRLS: Woman!

TEACHER: King John?

GIRLS: Woman!

TEACHER: Isaac Newton?

GIRLS: Woman!

TEACHER: Good! Good! Very, very good!

[*Class divides into groups. The repetition becomes rhythmic and possibly would involve gymnastics or more accurately 'physical jerks' of a tight and 'bound' nature*]

GROUP A: Shakeseare.

GROUP B: Woman.

GROUP C: Milton.

GROUP A: Woman.

GROUP B: Robin.

GROUP C: Woman.

GROUP A: Hood.

GROUP B: Woman.

GROUP C: King.

GROUP A: Woman.

GROUP B: John.

GROUP C: Woman.

GROUP A: Woman.

GROUP B: Woman.

GROUP C: Woman.

GROUP A: Woman.

GROUP B: Woman.

GROUP C: Woman.

GROUP A: Woman.

ALL: Woman, woman, woman, woman, woman, woman, woman.

TEACHER: Good! Good! Very, very good! Good! Good! Very, very good!

GIRL WHO WAS LATE: Tell us about men.

TEACHER [*outraged*]: Men!

ALL GIRLS: Men!

TEACHER: Men!

ALL GIRLS: Men!

TEACHER: Men are terrible, men are horrible, you're too young to know.

GIRLS: Please.

TEACHER: Men are black.

GIRLS [*with keen and growing interest, a thrill of horrified delight*]: Oh!

TEACHER: Men are thick.

GIRLS: Oh!

TEACHER: Men are tall.

GIRLS: Oh!

TEACHER: Men are strong.

GIRLS: Oh!

TEACHER: Men will beat you, tear you, eat you. When you're older you'll know.

[*Exit* TEACHER]

GIRLS [*two-two time. Thoughtfully to themselves*]: Men are black.
Men are thick.
Men are tall.
Men are strong.
Men will tear you, beat you, eat you.
When you're older, you will know.

[*The* GIRLS *take off their spectacles and loosen their hair. During the following repetition of the stamps, the spotlights come up in the section of the arena where* JOAN *and* STEPHEN *chased each other. Into each spotlight as it comes up there steps a* BOY. *The* GIRLS *as they repeat this stanza start to clap the rhythm gently and start to move with it. At first they do not see the* BOYS]

GIRLS [*six-eight time*]: Men are black.
Men are thick.
Men are tall.
Men are strong.
Men will tear you, beat you, eat you.
When you're older, you will know.

[*They turn, and now see the* BOYS. *There is a sense of awe, surprise, and wonder*]

Men are black.
Men are thick.

Men are tall.
Men are strong.
Men will tear you, beat you, eat you.
When you're older, you will know.

[*The* GIRLS *now continue a dance which is sustained by the
clapping rhythm they have already set up. The* BOYS *for
the moment do not move. In the next section of the dance the*
BOYS *and* GIRLS *dance together clapping, and the entire dance
finishes with the* GIRLS *and* BOYS *standing in pairs. Pause*]

1ST BOY [*holding out his hand*]: Bill.

1ST GIRL [*taking his hand*]: Jean.

2ND BOY [*holding out his hand*]: George.

2ND GIRL [*taking his hand*]: Anna.

3RD BOY [*holding out his hand*]: Mark.

3RD GIRL [*taking his hand*]: Miriam.

[*This business goes on until all the couples have joined hands
and given their names*]

BOYS AND GIRLS: The world cannot be divided.
The human race cannot be split.
What is a man without a woman?
What is a woman without a man?
Each needs the other.
Men and women.
Women and men.
Let us remember, a threat to all is a threat to each.
A threat to each is a threat to all.

[*As they speak, there is a movement around the entrances of
the arena which grows into a pressing and a creeping forward,*

*as hundreds of old women, silently bottling up their curiosity
and rage, elbow each other forward]*

OLD WOMEN [*whispering*]: Men! Men! Men! Men!

[*One of the* BOYS *runs forward and blows a whistle.
Immediately many more* BOYS *dash down the steps of the
auditorium and jump into the arena to join the others.
Meanwhile the* OLD WOMEN *with a cry of rage have fallen
on the first* BOY *and carried him away. They speedily erect
a pyre out of chairs (or a gibbet, and prepare to hang him, if
more suitable for stage arrangement) with a pole in the middle
against which they tie the* BOY *they have captured. Enter four*
CHARLADIES *with flaming mops. They start to set light to
the pyre. With a great cry the crowd of* BOYS *and* GIRLS
hurl themselves at the rabble of OLD WOMEN *and there
ensues a dance fight all over the arena, surging back and forth,
in which the* BOYS *and* GIRLS *are triumphant and finally chase
off the rabble]*

BOYS AND GIRLS [*triumphant*]: We won! We won! We won!

[*This becomes a joyful chant which grows into a dance and
climax.
At the other end of the arena, enter* MOTHER'S *travelling
pillar, surrounded by* CHARLADIES *with flaming mops,
cracking a great whip in her hand]*

MOTHER: You can never beat me. I can destroy the world.
Obey me, or I kill. [*She cracks her whip about her*] I can
destroy the world, obey me, or I kill. I can destroy the
world, obey me, or I kill.

[*The crowd of* BOYS *and* GIRLS *rush at her, but are kept off by
the flaming mops and the cracking whip]*

MOTHER: Yes! Yes! Now I will do it. Now! Now! Now! Ha! Ha! I'll show you. Ha! Right, right, all right! I'll show you. Do you know what I've got here? I'm old. I've got nothing to lose. I'll end the world. I long to die. I hate you. I'll finish you. I hate the world. I hate everything. Now let it happen. Now. Now.

[*A scream of jet engines, growing intensely loud. At first no movement in the arena*]

LOUDSPEAKER: Ten—nine—eight—seven. [*Continue counting through the following*]

[*The* OLD WOMEN *retreat to the exits*]

JOAN [*to the audience*]: White reflects heat. White reflects heat.

STEPHEN [*to the audience*]: Hold your programme in front of your face. White reflects heat. Hold your programme in front of your face!

LOUDSPEAKER: Hold your programme in front of your face.

LOUDSPEAKER: Six—five—four—three—two—

[*The young* GIRLS *(dressed in white) cluster round the* BOYS *and they hold out their exercise books with the white pages uppermost—in front of their faces and over their heads*]

LOUDSPEAKER: One—zero.

[BLACKOUT. *An intense and reverberating explosion. The explosion lingers. A quiet, precise voice, but the phrasing has poetic almost biblical overtones*]

LOUDSPEAKER: If a hydrogen bomb is dropped at Hyde Park Corner, there is a zone of instant death stretching from Southwark to Hammersmith. And for twenty miles round the centre of the explosion, say from Dorking to St. Albans, or Slough to Tilbury, there is damage varying in degree according to its distance from the centre of the explosion.

Nor is this all.
The fireball of the explosion which would endure for many seconds would cause vast fires which, driven by the great winds called forth by the changes in temperature, would burn what was not already destroyed.

Nor is this all.
So great would be the disruption and destruction, there would be little help for the survivors. Twelve bombs would destroy Great Britain and poison the world.

[*While the previous speech has been spoken, the arena has been lit to show spectre-like figures which stand still like dead trees in the quarter-light. The* VOICE *from the loudspeaker finishes. The sound of a child crying*]

THE SPECTRES: There is nothing, nothing left.
  That is not spoiled or broken.
  There is nothing, nothing left
  That is not spoiled or broken.
  The water is polluted,
  We cannot drink water.
  We cannot drink.

  There is nothing, nothing left.
  In one terrible flash
  The world we know has disappeared.
  Everything strange and dead.

  There is nothing, nothing left
  That is not spoiled or broken.

Rubble and a pile of ash.
Some smoking bricks,
Smell of fire.

[*Pause.*
Enter STEPHEN *at west end of the arena. He is also trying to trace the sound*]

STEPHEN: Where are you, where are you?

JOAN: Where are you?

[STEPHEN *sees* JOAN *and calls to her*]

STEPHEN: Joan!

[*They hold each other.*
The action has the effect of lightening and heartening the atmosphere, of calling the shadows back to life. There is a slight movement, a sigh from the shadowy figures. The lights begin to change to a warmer, brighter tone]

JOAN: We are alive!

[*The shadows are seen to be* BOYS *and* GIRLS]

ALL: We are alive!
We are alive! Yes!
See! We live! We breathe! We are not part of the destruction!
We are alive! Yes!
We are alive! Yes!
We are alive!

VOICE: I'm hungry.

ANOTHER VOICE: I want something to drink.

ANOTHER VOICE: The bomb has poisoned the earth.

[*Etc. Ad lib. in simplest, most direct, human way.
Pause*]

ALL: The bomb has poisoned the earth.

A VOICE: If we stay on earth we die.

ANOTHER VOICE: What shall we do?

[*Pause.
The following dialogue played with great directness and
simplicity—large statements interspersed with ad libbing
in which the statements are confirmed and digested*]

STEPHEN [*jumping on to a rostrum*]: We must leave the earth.

A VOICE: What?

STEPHEN AND JOAN: We must leave the earth.

[ALL *gather round* STEPHEN *and* JOAN *on the rostrum*]

ALL [*confused*]: What? What's he saying? Leave earth?

STEPHEN: A scientist! A scientist!

ALL [*loud and confused*]: A scientist? What's he want a scientist
for? Leave earth? *etc., etc., ad lib.*

STEPHEN: We must build a space ship!

[*Pause*]

ALL: A space ship! A space ship.

STEPHEN: A space ship.

[*Pause*]

ALL: A space ship.

STEPHEN: A scientist! Is there a scientist? Is there a scientist in
the house?

[*They all run to the barriers, up and down the stairs of the auditorium, asking for a scientist. Some shout from the middle of the arena, some speak direct to the audience*]

ALL: A scientist! Is there a scientist in the place? Excuse me, sir, are you a scientist? *etc., etc., ad lib.*

[*A man in a white coat is found in the auditorium. A great cheer from the young people. They take the scientist and carry him to the rostrum where he shakes hands with all of them*]

STEPHEN: Are you a scientist?

SCIENTIST: Well I've got my B.Sc. [*Cheers*]

STEPHEN: You must build us a space ship.

SCIENTIST: But—but [SCIENTIST *in a great flap is put back on to the rostrum*] I'm a chemist not a physicist.

VOICE: You got us into this mess. Now you get us out of it.

STEPHEN [*patiently and strongly*]: We must leave the earth.

SCIENTIST: You *must* leave earth?

STEPHEN: Yes.

SCIENTIST: Then you need a space ship.

ALL: A space ship.

SCIENTIST: I see. Well, I'll do my best, but I warn you, it won't·be easy. Very well. Now let's see. How big do you want it? That big? [*He gestures a sphere about eighteen inches in diameter*]

ALL: Not big enough.

SCIENTIST: Well—that big? [*Gesturing about a yard wide*]

ALL: Not big enough.

SCIENTIST: Not big enough! How big do you want it?

STEPHEN: Enough to take everyone left in the world.

SCIENTIST: All these people?

STEPHEN: All these and more.

[*A long pause*]

SCIENTIST: An entirely new principle!

ALL: Yes.

SCIENTIST: A flying saucer!

ALL: What?

SCIENTIST: A flying saucer. And I shall need some help.

[*Music. The* BOYS *and* GIRLS *divide into two groups.
One group gathers round the* SCIENTIST *who gives orders,
gesticulating. This group then splits up and exits in all
directions and there follows a purposeful sound of banging and
hammering and sawing followed by electronic noises, ticking,
whining, etc. Meanwhile* GROUP 2 *also exits but they
emerge into the auditorium where they run up and down the
stairs speaking directly to the audience*]

GROUP 2: We are leaving earth, We are leaving the dying
earth. You can come too, *etc., etc., ad lib.*

[*The audience should if possible be involved—relaying
instructions, passing objects etc.*
STEPHEN *and* JOAN *remain in the centre of the arena repeating
the same message into a microphone. There are now three
layers of activity: the banging, etc., in the passages outside the*

auditorium concerned with the building of the space ship, the
activities of GROUP 2 amongst the audience in the auditorium
and the amplified message coming from STEPHEN and JOAN
in the centre of the arena. This total activity rises to a climax.
Enter a small group of people.
STEPHEN starts to lead them to the edge of the arena. More
groups arrive and BOYS and GIRLS lead them to the edge of the
arena or out through the exits as if to take them up into the
auditorium. Above the banging and noise and the constantly
arriving groups of people there begins to come a sense of
purpose and order. STEPHEN with a hand microphone or
megaphone is organising]

STEPHEN: The group from Putney, will they please go to the
South Arena, Block 51. Edinburgh contingent, please go to
West Entrance A, rows A,B,C,D. Cardiff marshals, please
send Cardiff group to Entrance West D.

MARSHAL IN THE AUDITORIUM: This block is full, Steve.
West 32.

STEPHEN: Thank you, West 32 full. South Wales group,
please take your group to Entrance M North, rows F to K.

SECOND MARSHAL: Plenty of room here, Steve. Block 16
East.

STEPHEN: Good. Thank you. Block 16 East. How is it, South?

THIRD MARSHAL: South filling up, Steve.

STEPHEN: North?

FOURTH MARSHAL: North filling up, Steve.

STEPHEN: Then we shall have to use the arena. Scientist?

SCIENTIST: Yes?

STEPHEN: Will the weight bear?

SCIENTIST: I hope so. We must make everyone keep to the edges, to the edges. No weight in the middle—you see it must spin freely.

[*There has been a slight abatement in the people arriving, and now they start to come again. The arrivals become more formal (foreign groups) and possibly more decorative. These groups are marshalled to places in the arena*]

SCIENTIST: Too much weight in the middle. Too much weight here. The ship must spin, spin. There's too much weight in the middle. We must have weight at the edges. Weight at the edges will encourage the spin, otherwise I'm dreadfully afraid we shan't rise.

STEPHEN: The scientist says we must have weight at the edges. We'll have to get some of the people off the base here. Move along a little, please, the marshals will tell you. Thank you. Thank you.

[*Where possible, the marshals in the auditorium should actually move members of the audience closer together and put some of the cast in the extra seats. The central arena is cleared. The movable pillar is taken right to the middle of the arena, and the* SCIENTIST *starts to unroll a long cable to the central pillar. He then takes over the microphone from* STEPHEN]

SCIENTIST: Before we leave earth, here are one or two points. One: As the ship rises, the lights will go out. We need all the power we can get to raise this weight. Also you will feel the ship begin to spin. At first it may make you feel a little sick, but this will soon pass. As you feel it rising, press your feet well down and hold on to your seats. Now, please, I must ask you all to keep calm as the ship rises and to hold

tight. Now I must have somebody light in weight to start the ship. Everyone else must go to the rim. You will do.
[*This to* JOAN]

JOAN: Very well.
[*The* SCIENTIST *hands* JOAN *the cable*]

SCIENTIST: When you press this lever, the ship will rise.

JOAN: I see, press this.

SCIENTIST: Press it well down, and the ship will rise. Give us time to get to the edge.
[*They shake hands.*
Everyone but JOAN *now goes to the edge of the arena.*
JOAN *climbs to the top of the central pillar, taking the cable with her*]

JOAN: The ship must have a name. What shall we call the ship?

VOICE FROM AUDITORIUM: Mayflower.

2ND VOICE FROM AUDITORIUM: Ark.

3RD VOICE FROM AUDITORIUM: Hope.

ALL [*whispering*]: Hope. [*Murmuring to each other*] Hope.

JOAN: Let this ship be Hope. Close the doors!
[*Four great clanging sounds as of steel doors closing, from each of the four sides of the arena*]

JOAN: Now we leave earth and go outwards into the universe. When you leave this ship, when you walk out of the doors, it will be a new world, a different world.

ALL [*whispering*]: Ah. Yes!
[*Pause*]

JOAN: Are you ready? [*Pause*] Then rise, Hope.
C

[*She presses the lever. There starts a deep, throbbing hum, which gradually gathers force and intensity. As the noise increases, the lights slowly fade. The sound becomes sharper and sharper rising to the intense scream of jet engines. Music take over from the noise*]

THE END

As Good as New

DAVID PERRY

CAST

MRS PIMPLE
MR PIMBLE
MRS FLOWER
JUNE
SID

As Good as New

SCENE: *The living-room of the* PIMBLES' *basement flat near the district Underground station at Parson's Green.*
Two small windows in the room look out on to a flight of iron steps leading up to the street, just discernible through the top half of the windows. On the other side of the street is the railway embankment which carries the district line from Parson's Green to Putney Bridge.
Two doors lead into the room, one from the direction of the kitchen, the other from the bedrooms. The only entrance into the flat is down the iron staircase and round through a small yard to the kitchen door. In the kitchen are two doors, side by side: one leading into the bathroom and the other giving immediate access to a flight of stone steps leading to GRANDPA'S *workroom, formerly the cellar. The walls of the living-room are covered with glass cases containing various stuffed animals, mostly of a domestic nature. A table has been set for an elaborate tea.*
The curtain rises on MRS PIMBLE *at the sideboard. With the aid of a tea-spoon she is trying to extract a dead goldfish from its bowl. After deciding that she will never succeed in retrieving Sammy with the spoon she rushes to the table, picks up the sugar-tongs and finally manages to get him out of the bowl and on to a cushion on the sofa. She puts the tongs back in the sugar-bowl, forgetting to wipe them, and holds Sammy close to her ear, listening for heart-beats. Hearing nothing she shakes him violently but with even less response.*
SAMMY *to her horror is quite, quite dead.*

MRS PIMBLE [*calling in the direction of the bedrooms*]: Jack! Sammy's dead! [*No answer*] He's gone all stiff and funny. [*Still no answer*] Fat lot you care! [*Calling in the direction of the kitchen*] Grandma! Sammy's dead! What do you think I ought to do with him?

[*There is the sound of a lavatory chain being pulled*]

MRS PIMBLE [*muttering to herself*]: Poor little Sammy! It's all this hot weather. Kills 'em off something awful.

[MRS FLOWER *comes in from the kitchen*]

MRS PIMBLE: He's dead!

MRS FLOWER: Third one this year.

MRS PIMBLE: What am I going to do with him, Grandma? June'll be so upset. The very day she's bringing her young man home too.

MRS FLOWER: Better call Jack.

MRS PIMBLE: You know what he's like when he gets his head stuck into them comics. [*Calling*] Jack! Grandma says you've got to get up. There's been a death in the family. [*No answer*] Anyone would think *he* was dead for all the notice he takes. Well, we'll have to do something. [*Picking up the bowl*] Here, Grandma ... get rid of this down the sink ... [*giving her the fish*] ... and take Sammy to Grandpa. Where's he got to?

MRS FLOWER: He felt hot, so he's gone down the cellar to cool off.

MRS PIMBLE: Good, He can get to work on Sammy. Tell him to do a good job ... same as last time ... all nice and glossy. We'll hide the bowl and hope June doesn't notice. We don't want her going off into floods of tears with her young man coming.

MRS FLOWER: Late, isn't he?

MRS PIMBLE: June said four. It's already ten past. [*Calling*] Jack! It's ten past four! [*To* MRS FLOWER] Are you feeling better, Grandma?

MRS FLOWER [*like a shy girl*]: Oh, I'm all right now, dear.

MRS PIMBLE: That's right! Better to bring it up than to have it lying about on your chest.

[MRS FLOWER *goes into the kitchen. As she does so there is an ominous rumbling as a train passes overhead. All the glass cases rattle against the walls*]

MRS PIMBLE: Jack! Have you forgotten June's bringing her young man to tea? The Upminster's just gone by. The next Wimbledon'll be here in ten minutes' time. So you'd better stir yourself. [*No answer*] Are you listening to me?

MR PIMBLE [*off, from the bedroom*]: Eh?

MRS PIMBLE: Put that comic away and get your best trousers on. It's ten past four and time you was up. [*Hearing a noise from the kitchen*] Careful how you go down them cellar-steps, Grandma!

MR PIMBLE [*off*]: What's she doing down there?

MRS PIMBLE: She's taking Sammy down to Grandpa.

MR PIMBLE [*off*]: What on earth for?

MRS PIMBLE: Because he's dead. [*As* MR PIMBLE *coughs violently*] You'd better have one of your lozenges. June won't want you coughing all over the tea-table. [*To herself,*

counting the places round the tea-table] There's me ... Father
... Grandma ... June ... and Mr ... Mr ... [*Going into
the kitchen and calling*] Grandma! What's June's young man
called?

[*There is the sound of muffled voices from the cellar*]

MRS FLOWER [*off, from the cellar*]: Grandpa says it's Leslie
Moon, dear.

MRS PIMBLE: Leslie Moon my foot! He was the last one. No,
it's Sidney something. Sidney Lovejoy!

[MRS FLOWER *enters from the kitchen*]

MRS PIMBLE: Grandpa getting on with it, is he?

MRS FLOWER: He's always a bit slow on fish. They take a bit
of skinning. You've laid forks, dearie.

MRS PIMBLE: Yes, I thought we'd start off with a tin of salmon.
Though I don't know about you, Grandma. Do you think
you ought to risk it?

MRS FLOWER [*not wishing to answer*]: I'll put the kettle on.

MRS PIMBLE [*as MRS FLOWER goes into the kitchen*]: Grandpa
can have his downstairs on a tray. You know how he hates
being interrupted when he's got a job on. [*Calling*] Jack!
Have you gone back to bed again?

MR PIMBLE [*off*]: I can't find my lozenges.

MRS PIMBLE: Last time I saw them they was on top of one of
the cases. Tiny Tim, I think it was. Oh, and that reminds
me, Jack! Whatever you do, don't mention anything about
Sammy. We don't want any upsets while Mr Lovejoy's
here. You know what June's like. [*Looking at a vase of sorry-*

looking flowers on the mantelpiece] These flowers look half-dead.

MRS FLOWER [*coming in from the kitchen*]: That's done, dear.

MRS PIMBLE: Oh, thank you, Grandma. Nothing lasts this weather. Even Jack looks fit to drop.

MRS FLOWER: Don't feel too bright myself, dear.

MRS PIMBLE: Well, Grandma, can you wonder? Look at you at dinner-time. I've never seen anybody put away so much.

MRS FLOWER [*like a little girl*]: You know how much I like a nice bit of pork.

MRS PIMBLE: What good does it do you when you bring it all up again half an hour later? Now don't you go bolting your tea. We want to create a good impression with this young man. After all, June's nearly thirty-five now and she won't get many more chances. It's now or never, if you ask me.

MR PIMBLE [*coming in from the bedroom*]: What is?

MRS PIMBLE: June getting married.

MR PIMBLE: She'll be lucky!

MRS PIMBLE: Now, Jack, that's very unfair. We all know that June's a bit on the plain side but this young man's very fond of her.

MR PIMBLE [*nodding towards the glass cases*]: Does he know about all this carry-on?

MRS PIMBLE: Shouldn't think so. June's not daft.

MR PIMBLE: He'll have to know sooner or later.

MRS PIMBLE: Time enough when he's one of the family. June knows what she's doing.

MR PIMBLE: She thought she knew what she was doing with Leslie Moon.

MRS PIMBLE [*sharply*]: All that was a long time ago. Besides it wasn't June's fault. If Leslie Moon hadn't gone barging down the cellar-steps none of that need ever have happened. Poor Grandpa nearly threw a fit. As for June, I never thought she'd stop crying.

MR PIMBLE [*wearily*]: Bloomin' wet week-end that was.

MRS PIMBLE: Never mind. In some ways it all worked out for the best. You know how upset she used to get at the thought of being called June Moon. [*Sharply, as* MRS FLOWER *heaves with laughter*] Grandma! Go and wash the lettuce! I left it soaking in the bowl. [*As* MRS FLOWER *shuffles into the kitchen*] And you can pop out into the yard and give the outside leaves to Delia. It'll do that poor little rabbit good to see a bit of green stuff.

MR PIMBLE [*who has settled down into an armchair with his comic*]: Where's he coming from?

MRS PIMBLE: Earls Court. June says he's got ever such a nice little bed-sit. All bright and gay with big windows.

MR PIMBLE: That's the sort of place I'd like. I'm getting a bit fed up with this, you know, Hetty. I was lying in bed just now, looking at the walls. Nothing but cases of stuffed animals from floor to ceiling. Can't we get rid of them?

MRS PIMBLE: You try suggesting that to June.

MR PIMBLE [*sighing*]: Well, I don't know. It makes the place so stuffy. I'm sure it's that what's given me a bad chest.

MRS PIMBLE: You smoke too much, that's your trouble.

MRS FLOWER [*poking her head round the kitchen door*]: What about the salmon? Shall I open up the tin?

MRS PIMBLE: Oh, yes, please, Grandma. Turn it out into a bowl and put a drop of vinegar over it. [*As* MRS FLOWER *retreats into the kitchen*] Oh, and Grandma ... don't pick!

MR PIMBLE: Don't know how she's stood it all these years.

MRS PIMBLE: She's all right all the time Grandpa's cheerful.

MR PIMBLE: He's the fly in the ointment, if you ask me.

MRS PIMBLE [*sharply*]: What do you mean by that?

MR PIMBLE: Well, if he hadn't started this taxidermy nonsense we shouldn't all be living in this mess. Every time I go down to that cellar it makes my stomach turn.

MRS PIMBLE [*on her dignity*]: Well, I think it's rather wonderful for an old man like him to have an interesting hobby. Where would we be with June now, if he hadn't been there to do up all her pets as good as new?

MR PIMBLE [*vehemently*]: It's unhealthy, that's what it is! June's old enough to realise that when something's dead and gone it's dead and gone ... and that's all there is to it. You can't go on preserving things for ever.

MRS PIMBLE: That's not fair, Jack! June's always loved animals but somehow she's just been unlucky with them. You can't blame her for getting a bit sentimental.

MR PIMBLE: That's no reason why she should have them stuffed and put in glass cases. It's like living in a museum. What's more, it puts me clean off my food.

MRS FLOWER [*poking her head round the kitchen door*]: Kettle's
boiling, dear. Shall I make a cup while we're waiting?

MRS PIMBLE: Might as well, Grandma. And you'd better take
a cup down to Grandpa too. I expect he could do with one.
[*To* MR PIMBLE] I do hope he does a good job on Sammy.
He always has terrible trouble with fish.

MR PIMBLE [*with great sympathy*]: Poor little blighter!
Couldn't have been much fun living in a bowl.

MRS PIMBLE: It's this dreadful hot weather that 'did' for him.
Even poor little Delia doesn't know what to do with herself
out in that hutch. Never known an August like it.

MR PIMBLE [*with infinite longing*]: I wish we could have gone
away somewhere this year. Bognor would have been nice.

MRS FLOWER [*coming in from the kitchen with two cups*]:
When I took him down his tea he said somebody'll have to
go up to that shop in town 'cause he's running out of eyes.
Here's your tea, Jack.

MR PIMBLE: Ta.

MRS PIMBLE [*choking over her tea*]: Here, Grandma, do you
want to kill me? You've gone and put sugar in it, you silly
daft ha'porth! And me with my diabetes!

MRS FLOWER: Sorry, dearie. Jack must have got yours.

MRS PIMBLE [*swapping cups*]: I don't want to go getting them
dizzy spells again. Been feeling a lot better lately, touch
wood. [*To* GRANDMA *who is holding an imaginary cup*]
Where's your cup, Grandma?

MRS FLOWER: Cup, dear? [*Looking at her hands*] Oh! I thought
I had it in my hand. I must have left it in the kitchen.

MRS PIMBLE [*as* GRANDMA *exits*]: She doesn't know what she's doing half the time.

[*A train rumbles overhead and all the glass cases rattle against the wall*]

MRS PIMBLE: That's the Wimbledon! [*Snatching up the cups and dashing into the kitchen*] Grandma! That was the Wimbledon! [*Off*] Grandma! Where are you? [*Dashing back into the living-room*] Where's Grandma?

MR PIMBLE [*coughing his heart up*]: How the blazes should I know?

[*There is the sound of a chain being pulled*]

MRS PIMBLE [*off*]: Grandma! Have you been bad again? I told you to keep your fingers off the salmon, didn't I? [*Propelling* MRS FLOWER *into a chair in the sitting-room*] I'll never forgive you if you go spoiling things for June. Now sit down and pull yourself together. [*To* MR PIMBLE] Jack! I do wish you wouldn't smoke so much. [*Suddenly becoming dictatorial*] Now listen to me, both of you. In a couple of minutes' time there's going to be a young man walk down them steps. That young man's going to be June's husband if I know anything about it. He's going to lead my June up to the altar and he's going to say 'I will' in a good loud voice. So I want you both to go out of your way to be nice to him. And if anyone mentions Leslie Moon they'll get what-for in a big way.

MRS FLOWER [*vacantly*]: Who's Leslie Moon, dear?

MRS PIMBLE: Oh, Grandma, do wake up! Leslie Moon was the one what fell down the cellar-steps.

MRS FLOWER [*laughing happily*]: Oh, that one!

MR PIMBLE: Poor little blighter!

MRS FLOWER: Thought he was opening up the door into the bathroom, didn't he? Landed up in the cellar instead.

MRS PIMBLE [*severely*]: That's enough, Grandma.

MRS FLOWER [*ceasing abruptly*]: Yes, dear. [*Lugubriously*] That was the best laugh we'd had in years.

[*Through the window* JUNE *and* SID *can be seen descending the iron staircase into the yard*]

JUNE [*waving through the window*]: Coooo–eeee! [*Indicating* SID *who has a bird-cage in one hand and roses in the other*] This is my Sid. He's bought me a linnet. Haven't you, Sid?

MRS FLOWER [*as* JUNE *and* SID *disappear from view*]: What's he bought her?

MRS PIMBLE: A linnet.

MRS FLOWER: What's that?

MRS PIMBLE: A little bird what sings.

MR PIMBLE: Oh, Christmas!

[MRS PIMBLE *shoots him a vicious glance. There is a pause.* JUNE *and* SID *can be heard talking in the yard*]

MRS FLOWER [*to* MRS PIMBLE]: Why don't they come in, dear?

MRS PIMBLE: Perhaps he's frightened to.

MRS PIMBLE: Why should he be frightened to, you daft ha'porth! Anyone would think we was going to eat him.

MR PIMBLE: 'Ere, 'ere!

MRS PIMBLE: Well, I'm nervous.

MR PIMBLE [*triumphant*]: I thought you was the one what was going to be all calm and dignified.

JUNE [*entering*]: Mum!

MRS PIMBLE: Yes, dear?

JUNE: Sid says that June's little Delia looks a bit poorly. Haven't you got any lettuce?

MRS PIMBLE: Didn't you give her the outside leaves like I told you, Grandma?

MRS FLOWER: I forgot, dear.

MRS PIMBLE: Go and do it this instant!

MRS FLOWER [*going to the kitchen-door and colliding with* SID *coming in*]: Ooooh, I say!

SID: Oh, I beg your pardon!

JUNE [*coming to the rescue*]: Oh, Grandma, this is Sid.

SID: How do you do?

MRS FLOWER [*staring at him with a sort of vacant alarm*]: You'd better find out where the bathroom is before you start.

JUNE [*as* MRS FLOWER *goes into the kitchen*]: What's come over Grandma?

MRS PIMBLE: It's the hot weather, dear. [*Going up to* SID] How do you do, Mr Lovejoy? I'm June's mother.

SID: Pleased to meet you, Mrs Pimble.

JUNE: Sid, this is Dad.

MR PIMBLE [*affably*]: How do you do, son?

SID: Nicely, thanks.

JUNE [*looking round*]: Mum, where's Grandpa?

MRS PIMBLE [*quickly*]: Grandpa, dear? Oh, he'll be up presently. He's doing a little job down in the cellar.

JUNE: What little job, Mum?

MRS PIMBLE: Having a tidy-up, I think. Isn't he, Jack? Look, aren't you going to ask Mr Lovejoy to sit down, June dear?

JUNE: Oh, I say! Just look at poor Sid standing there holding June's little Ruby. [*Taking the cage from him and putting it on the sideboard*] You can all have a peep in a minute when I get the brown paper off. [*Coming back to* SID *and taking the roses*] Oh, Mum! Sid bought you a bunch of roses, didn't you, Sid? [*Giving them back to him*] Go on, Sid! You give them to Mum.

SID [*doing so*]: I bought you a bunch of roses, Mrs Pimble.

MRS PIMBLE [*cooing*]: Oh, now isn't that nice! Oh, do look, Jack! Mmmmmm, aren't they lovely!

MR PIMBLE [*wistfully*]: Makes me think of gardens.

MRS PIMBLE: A nice bokay like that makes me think of weddings. [*Calling*] Grandma!

MRS FLOWER [*off*]: Yes, dear?

MRS PIMBLE: Be a dear and put these into water. You'll find a jug in the cupboard. [*As* MRS FLOWER *takes them*] Have you fed Delia now, Grandma?

MRS FLOWER [*going back into the kitchen*]: Yes, dearie. She didn't half perk up.

MRS PIMBLE: Yes, well, I daresay Mr Lovejoy could do with something to perk him up too. What about a nice cup of tea, Mr Lovejoy?

SID: Thanks very much.

MRS PIMBLE [*calling*]: Grandma'll put the kettle on, won't you, Grandma? [*In her brightest social manner*] Well, won't you sit down, Mr Lovejoy, and make yourself at home?

SID [*sitting*]: Thanks, I will.

MRS PIMBLE: June's told us ever such a lot about you. Hasn't she, Jack?

MR PIMBLE [*enviously*]: She told us you've got a nice bright room with big window. Bet it's not as stuffy as it is down here.

MRS PIMBLE [*sharply*]: Jack! [*By way of explanation*] Mr Pimble suffers with his chest, you know. [*Changing conversation*] Train was late, wasn't it, love?

JUNE: They're doing something to the line outside West Brompton. Oh, Mum! It was embarrassing. The train was held up for ages and it was ever so crowded. And you know how people seem to go all quiet when they're packed together like sardines and nothing's happening. Well, the train stopped and nobody said anything . . . when all of a sudden Ruby starts singing.

MR PIMBLE: Who's Ruby?

JUNE: June's linnet. Singing at the top of her voice she was, like as if she was at Covent Garden, and pecking at the brown paper and kicking up a terrible row—wasn't she, Sid?

SID: Yes.

JUNE: Poor Sid didn't know where to put his face, 'cause he had her on his lap, see, and everybody was staring. Well, all of a sudden I began to see the funny side of it, what with all them people standing there like statues, just gawping. Tell 'em what I did, Sid.

SID: She giggled.

JUNE: Honest. I sat there laughing till the tears streamed down my face. And the louder Ruby sang the more I giggled—didn't I, Sid?

SID: Then the trained jerked forward and everyone fell over.

JUNE: Right on top of Ruby. Talk about laugh. I nearly died.

MR PIMBLE: What did you want to wrap it up in brown paper for?

SID [*laughing*]: Because the chap where we bought her said that if you did that it stopped 'em singing.

JUNE [*shrieking*]: Yes, he did, didn't he, Sid? Still, perhaps when the train stopped she thought she'd got home. [*Bringing the cage over to the table*] You wait till you see her. Ever so perky she is, and the tiniest bird you ever saw. You undo it, Sid. I can't manage all this string.

MR PIMBLE: She's not singing very much now, is she?

JUNE: You wait till we have the brown paper off. She'll be rushing about that cage like nobody's business. [*To* SID *who is now removing the brown paper*] Careful how you go now, Sid. Do it gradual. We don't want her flying off into a panic with all the family standing round staring.

SID: Gently does it.

JUNE [*wheedling*]: Is June's little Ruby going to sing·us a little song?

MR PIMBLE: Shouldn't think so, if you talk to her like that.

SID [*removing the paper which* MRS PIMBLE *takes and puts on the sofa*]: Blow me!

JUNE: What's up, Sid?

SID: She's hopped it.

JUNE: She can't have.

SID: Well, I can't see her.

MR PIMBLE: I can.

JUNE: Where, Dad?

MR PIMBLE [*pointing*]: Down here in the corner.

SID: Yes, she's there right enough. Down in the corner.

JUNE: She's frightened.

SID: If you ask me, she's poorly.

MRS PIMBLE: She's not moving very much.

JUNE [*as* SID *opens the cage door and takes out the linnet*]: Oh dear, oh dear! I do hope nothing's wrong. Perhaps she's gone and fainted.

SID [*looking closely*]: It's worse than that, love.

JUNE [*in a tiny voice*]: What do you mean, Sid?

SID: I'm afraid she's dead.

MRS PIMBLE [*with horror*]: Dead?

SID: She's as stiff as a board.

[*There is an awful pause as they all take it in. Then out of the silence comes a thin wail, always the prelude to one of* JUNE's *crises. Immediately* MRS PIMBLE *is galvanised into activity.* MR PIMBLE *has a severe fit of coughing.* SID *just looks bewildered and stands holding the dead bird*]

MRS PIMBLE: Oh dear, oh dear! I don't know what's wrong with this house, honest I don't. Jack! For Heaven's sake stop coughing and give me a hand with June. She'd better go and have a lay-down while she gets over it. Of course this would happen with Mr Lovejoy coming to tea.

SID: It's not your fault, Mrs Pimble.

JUNE [*wailing*]: It's Fate, that's what it is! Fate's come and taken away June's little Ruby.

MR PIMBLE: You can't expect anything else if you wrap a bird up in brown paper this weather.

MRS PIMBLE: Jack!

MR PIMBLE: Well, it stands to reason. I'd like to see how long you lasted, all done up in a parcel.

JUNE [*shrieking*]: How were we to know she was feeling poorly? She was chirping away like anything in the chube. Singing her swan-song, that's what she was. Giving us all a chune with her dying gasp.

MRS PIMBLE [*greatly distressed*]: Oh, June, don't take on so!

JUNE: Fate's taken away my Ruby and left me with an empty cage!

MR PIMBLE: Oh, Christmas!

MRS PIMBLE: Shut up, Jack, and help me get her to her room. [*To* SID] You just sit down, Mr Lovejoy, and make yourself at home. Come along now, June, there's a good girl. Mum's going to take you for a little lay-down.

JUNE: Dead, that's what she is! Dead and gone!

MRS PIMBLE [*leading her off, helped by* MR PIMBLE]: Now don't you go worrying about that, love. Mum's going to take Ruby down to Grandpa and get him to fix her up again as good as new. Before you know where you are we'll have her looking all bright and perky in a nice glass case.

[MR *and* MRS PIMBLE *go off with a howling* JUNE. *Left alone,* SID *gulps and stares round the room, taking in all the glass cases with an expression of absolute bewilderment. As he is looking at them a train passes overhead and they all rattle against the wall. After a pause* MRS FLOWER *comes in from the kitchen and, without* SID *noticing, stands looking at him.*]

MRS FLOWER [*like a shy girl*]: Hullo, dear. You're going to marry our June, aren't you?

SID [*taken aback*]: Well, it's not really official yet, Mrs . . . er?

MRS FLOWER: Flower. The sort you pick, not the sort you make pastry with.

SID: It's not really official yet, Mrs Flower. 'Course we've been going steady for quite a while now.

MRS FLOWER: June's nearly thirty-five, you see, and she won't get many more chances.

SID [*good naturedly*]: Well, I'm no chicken myself, if it comes to that.

MRS FLOWER [*giggling*]: Seems funny to hear you say that, Mr Lovejoy. I bet you'd never guess how old I am. [*Confidentially*] Seventy-nine next birthday.

SID: Seventy-nine's a grand age.

MRS FLOWER [*with another giggle*]: Not really. You wait till you meet Grandpa. He's ninety-seven.

SID [*genuinely surprised*]: Ninety-seven! June never told me.

MRS FLOWER: 'Course, he can't get about like he used to.

SID: Where is he now? Is he still tidying up?

MRS FLOWER [*heaving with laughter*]: Tidying up? Lord, no! Grandpa never does no tidying up. No. He's down the cellar. It's nice and cool down there, you see. Has to be for his work.

SID: Whatever does he do?

MRS FLOWER: He stuffs.

SID: Stuffs?

MRS FLOWER: Yes, animals and things. He's a taxidermist.

SID [*looking round the walls*]: Oh, I see. And how long's he been doing this for, Mrs Flower?

MRS FLOWER: Ever since he retired.

SID: And what was he before that?

MRS FLOWER: He was a keeper at the London Zoo. Elephants mostly. Very upset he was when he had to retire. He missed his animals, you see. We had a terrible time with him at first.

SID: How was that, Mrs Flower?

MRS FLOWER [*expanding*]: Well, he used to fret, see? All day long he'd sit around moping. Then one day Hetty . . . that's Mrs Pimble . . . she went and fetched the doctor to him and he said the best thing he could do would be to take up a hobby, something to occupy his mind.

SID: So he started on this, did he?

MRS FLOWER: Not straight away. It was very queer how it come about. [*Suddenly becoming doubtful*] I don't know if Hetty would like me telling you all this.

SID [*smiling*]: She won't mind if I'm going to be one of the family.

MRS FLOWER [*giggling*]: That's what she's hoping. . . . Well, dearie, it all started with June's Teddy Bear. June was only a little girl in them days and as pretty as a picture. Well, she had a Teddy Bear what Jack bought her . . . that's Mr Pimble . . . and she thought the world of it. Anyway, one day something happened to it and it all fell to pieces. Talk about straw . . . it was all over the carpet! And there was poor June sitting in the middle of it all and howling her head off. Well, next day Grandpa goes off and buys some wadding, and without telling nobody, takes the Teddy Bear to pieces and does it up again as good as new. Lovely job he made of it, with all neat stitches where the seams was. You should have seen June's face when he gave it to her. Lord! We shan't ever forget that Teddy Bear. She still has it in bed with her even now.

SID: So that's what it was that gave Mr Flower the idea to try it out on the real thing, I suppose?

MRS FLOWER: Well, it must have been. Next thing we knew he was off round Fulham Library reading up books on taxidermy, him as had read nothing but comics all his life.

SID: Taxidermy sounds a very complicated business, Mrs Flower.

MRS FLOWER: Oh, it is, Mr Lovejoy! Took him ages to learn. First time he tried he made a proper muck-up of one of our cats. Poor thing finished up looking as if something had hit it. [*Heaving with laughter*]

MRS PIMBLE [*coming in from the direction of the bedroom*]: There you are, Grandma. [*To* SID] What poor Mr Lovejoy must think of us, I dread to think. Haven't you made him a cup of tea, Grandma?

MRS FLOWER: Kettle hasn't boiled yet, dear.

SID: How's June, Mrs Pimble?

MRS PIMBLE: She'll be all right when she's had a lay-down. She always gets a bit upset when anything like this happens. It's the price you pay for being so sensitive, I suppose. [*To* MRS FLOWER] Now then, Grandma, I want you to take Ruby down to Grandpa. Tell him to put Sammy on one side and make a start on her right away. June says she wants her with her beak open like as if she was singing. [*To* SID] Our Grandpa's very clever with his hands, Mr Lovejoy.

SID: So I've just been hearing, Mrs Pimble.

MRS PIMBLE [*suspiciously*]: Grandma been talking to you, has she?

MRS FLOWER: We had a few words, didn't we, Mr Lovejoy?

MRS PIMBLE: Well, now you can get on and make him a cup of tea. [*Giving her the linnet*] Here you are then, Grandma. And mind how you go down them cellar-steps.

[MRS FLOWER *goes into the kitchen as* MR PIMBLE *comes in from the direction of the bedrooms*]

MR PIMBLE: June says she's going to get up.

MRS PIMBLE: Oh, Jack, she mustn't!

MR PIMBLE: Well, you try stopping her. As soon as your back was turned she was out of that bed like greased lightning and putting on her black.

MRS PIMBLE [*exploding*]: What? For a dead linnet that ain't no bigger than a ping-pong ball? Mr Lovejoy's going to think she's off her head!

SID [*as* MRS PIMBLE *rushes off*]: I've never known June to be quite like this before.

MR PIMBLE: You haven't seen half of it yet, son. [*Noticing* SID's *bewilderment*] What's the matter? You look a bit hot.

SID: Yes, it's not as cool as it might be.

MR PIMBLE: Never known an August like it. [*Rolling a cigarette*] Like me to roll you a fag, son?

SID: No, thanks, Mr Pimble. I don't smoke.

MR PIMBLE: Don't know how you manage it. It's the only thing what keeps me going.

SID: Well, it's doctor's orders really. I had a spell in hospital when I was a lad.

MR PIMBLE: Got something wrong with you, have you? You've come to the right place here then. We haven't got a ha'porth of good health between us. What's wrong with you?

SID [*laughing*]: I've got a funny heart.

MR PIMBLE: Sounds like it. What's the matter with it?

SID: Well, two things really. To begin with it's on this side and not on that.

MR PIMBLE: Blow me! That's bad enough. What's the other thing? Hey, you're not going to tell me it's upside-down, I hope?

SID [*laughing*]: No. But it's twice as big as anybody else's.

MR PIMBLE: Christmas! Here, what does it feel like having a heart as big as that on the wrong side?

SID: It doesn't feel any different from anybody else. I get a bit winded if I get worked up, but apart from that I'm as fit as a fiddle. In fact, if I take it easy enough there's no reason why I shouldn't live till I'm ninety-seven, like Mr Flower.

MRS PIMBLE [*coming in from the direction of the bedrooms*]: June says she's all right now and we're all to carry on as if nothing had happened. As soon as she comes I think we'd best have tea. She's just having a tidy-up in the mirror and putting on a new face.

MR PIMBLE: Spoilt Mr Lovejoy's afternoon properly this has. [*Suddenly remembering*] Here, Hetty, he's just been telling me he's got a heart twice as big as anybody else's.

MRS PIMBLE: Needs to have with June in this mood. Where's Grandma?

SID: I think she was taking Ruby down to Mr Flower, Mrs Pimble.

MRS PIMBLE: Hasn't she made that tea yet? [*Calling into the kitchen*] Grandma! What do you think you're doing with that tea?

[*There is the sound of a chain being pulled*]

MRS PIMBLE [*collapsing into a chair*]: Jack, I give up! I've only got to turn my back for five minutes and she goes helping

herself to the sherry-trifle. I don't know, honest I don't.
I do my best to make things all nice and welcome for
Mr Lovejoy and everything goes wrong.

MR PIMBLE: We'll all sit down and have a quiet tea when
June comes. Everyone'll feel better when they've had something to eat.

[JUNE *comes in from the direction of the bedrooms. She has
changed into a black dress and looks suitably pale*]

JUNE [*in a thin voice*]: June's hungry.

MRS PIMBLE [*leaping up*]: Oh, there you are, June! Are you all
right now, love? You'd better come and have a sit-down
while Mum sees to the tea. It doesn't look as if Grandma's
going to be much use one way and another.

JUNE [*spotting the bird-cage where it was left on the table*]: Mum!
I wish you'd taken Ruby's cage off the table 'stead of it
sitting up there like a coffin.

MRS PIMBLE [*to* MRS FLOWER *as she comes in from the kitchen*]:
Grandma! Couldn't you have done something about getting
rid of Ruby's cage?

MRS FLOWER: I been down the cellar, dear.

MRS PIMBLE: Then do something about it now. We don't
want to be reminded of Ruby all through tea. [*Suddenly
remembering*] Here, what happened to them lovely roses
Mr Lovejoy bought for me? Didn't you put them in water
like I told you?

MRS FLOWER: Yes, dear. I left 'em on the draining-board.

MRS PIMBLE: Well, bring them in here, Grandma. Why have

them staring into the sink when they'll make a nice centre-piece for the tea-table? How's Grandpa getting on?

MRS FLOWER [*going into the kitchen with the bird-cage*]: He's all right, dear. Last time I went down he was whistling.

SID: Will it take him very long, Mrs Pimble?

MRS PIMBLE: Lord, yes! It's a dreadful paraphernalia. Twisting bits of wire about and building bodies out of balsa-wood. That cellar looks like a battlefield some days.

MRS FLOWER [*coming back with the flowers*]: Shall I put them on the table, dear?

JUNE [*shrieking*]: Oh, Mum!

MRS PIMBLE: What's the matter now, June?

JUNE: Grandma's gone and put them roses in Sammy's goldfish bowl. She'll suffocate him. [*Snatching the flowers out of the bowl*] He's gone! [*Shrieking*] Grandma, what have you done with him? What have you done with my Sammy?

MRS PIMBLE [*exploding*]: Grandma, you daft ha'porth! What did I tell you? Haven't you got any more sense than to go putting roses in a goldfish bowl?

MRS FLOWER: Sorry dear. I forgot.

MRS PIMBLE: You forgot? Here have I been doing my best to keep it from her and you say you forgot.

JUNE: What do you mean, Mum? What's happened?

MRS FLOWER: He's gone down to Grandpa, dearie.

JUNE: What do you mean, 'He's gone down to Grandpa'?

MRS FLOWER: He's stopped moving.

MRS PIMBLE [*cutting in sharply*]: She means he's dead!

[*There is an awful pause while the truth sinks in. Out of the silence comes* JUNE's *thin wail*]

MRS PIMBLE: Oh dear, oh dear! Now what have I said? I don't know what's wrong with this place, honest I don't. Strikes me we've got evil spirits in the floor-boards. Jack, give me a hand with June. She'd better go back to her bedroom for another lay-down.

JUNE [*howling*]: It's Fate, that's what it is! Fate's come along and taken away June's little Sammy.

MR PIMBLE: Oh, Christmas!

JUNE: He was the happiest little goldfish ever to swim round a bowl . . .

MRS PIMBLE: Come along now, June.

JUNE: . . . And Grandma goes and puts roses in it like as if she was sprinkling flowers on a watery grave!

MRS PIMBLE: Now don't you worry about Sammy, love. You just leave everything to Grandpa. Before you know where you are he'll have him looking all new and glossy in a nice glass case.

[MR *and* MRS PIMBLE *lead* JUNE *off in the direction of the bed-rooms*]

MRS FLOWER [*looking at* SID *who has been considerably shaken by the turn of events*]: You're looking flushed, dearie.

SID [*mopping his brow*]: Yes, I am feeling a bit hot.

MRS FLOWER: Gets like an oven down here in the summer. When we had that dreadful heat-wave back in forty-seven we all moved down into the cellar along with Grandpa. Proper god-send that cellar's been one way and another. [*Darkly*] 'Course, it's seen its share of tragedy too, you know.

SID: Tragedy, Mrs Flower?

MRS FLOWER: Though we don't talk about it much any more. Hetty says as we was all to go on as if nothing had happened. 'Course I'm not supposed to say anything really. But I don't suppose it matters if you're going to be one of the family. [*Noticing that* SID *is looking doubtful*] You're not having second thoughts, are you?

SID: What makes you say that, Mrs Flower?

MRS FLOWER: Well, you don't look quite so perky as when you first come in.

SID: It's just that I'm a little upset by all that's happened, that's all. I've never seen June like this until today.

MRS FLOWER: That's cos you've never seen her at home before. [*Mysteriously*] I suppose she didn't tell you nothing about Leslie Moon, did she dearie?

SID: Who's he?

MRS FLOWER [*giggling*]: June's young man as used to be. The one what fell all the way down the cellar-steps.

MRS PIMBLE [*entering and crossing into the kitchen*]: June wants a glass of water. With any luck she'll pull round in time to join us all for tea.

MRS FLOWER [*continuing in an awful whisper*]: Right the way down the cellar-steps from top to bottom. Left a lump on the back of his head the size of a duck's egg. One of the nastiest falls I've ever seen. And him as used to be a para-chutist!

MRS PIMBLE [*off, from the kitchen*]: Grandma!

MRS FLOWER [*starting guiltily*]: Yes, dear?

MRS PIMBLE [*off*]: Not only has the kettle boiled dry but you've been and left the back-door open, you daft ha'porth!

MRS FLOWER: I thought we could all do with some fresh air, dearie.

MRS PIMBLE [*coming in with a glass of water*]: Oh, did you? Well, you can try doing something right for a change and take this glass of water along to June's bedroom. [*Hustling* MRS FLOWER *out of the room*] And for your information the blow-flies have been at the salmon! [*Coming back into the living-room*] Mr Lovejoy, I don't know how to apologise, really I don't. Nothing's gone right since breakfast. I wanted a nice quiet day with everybody sitting round enjoying themselves and all I've done is run round in circles.

SID: I hope it isn't always like this for you, Mrs Pimble.

MRS PIMBLE: Oh, we have our ups and downs, I suppose. [*Seeing her chance*] Be a bit better when we've got June off our hands, I expect.

SID: I was just saying to Mrs Flower that I'd never seen June like this before.

MRS PIMBLE [*suspiciously*]: Grandma been talking to you, has she?

SID: Yes, we did have a little chat just now.

MRS PIMBLE: I hope she hasn't been saying things about our June?

SID: What sort of things?

MRS PIMBLE: Well, things to make you wonder. She's got a funny habit of telling people only half a story. Always done it ever since I can remember.

SID: I've heard all about Mr Flower and his taxidermy, if that's what you mean. Mr Pimble was telling me about that as well.

MRS PIMBLE: Jack was? Don't you believe a word he says, Mr Lovejoy. Never content with what he's got, that's his trouble. Mind you, I'm not saying he's been a bad husband to me, cos he hasn't. Trouble with my Jack is he's never had no 'go'. I like a man with a bit of push and shove who knows what he wants. Jack just sits down and dreams and ends up where he started. Still, as I say to Grandma, that's what comes of spending a lifetime driving trains on the Inner Circle.

SID [*embarrassed*]: Well, if it comes to that, Mrs Pimble, I suppose I haven't got a very exciting job myself. There's not much future in being an orderly in Hammersmith Hospital.

MRS PIMBLE: No, but June tells me you do lots of studying at night school. That's what I like to see—someone with ambition. That's why my June's always been choosey with her boy-friends. I've brought her up to look for quality in a man, Mr Lovejoy. Quality. I don't want her rushing into any old marriage. [*Pointedly*] 'June,' I said, 'don't you throw yourself away, love. Just you wait until Mr Right comes along—even if it means hanging on till your thirty-five.'

SID: Well, I've always been on the cautious side myself,

Mrs Pimble. I think you have to know a person inside-out before you start committing yourself to a life partnership.

MRS PIMBLE [*forced to agree*]: Quite right too, Mr Lovejoy. It's not a good thing to wait too long, though. Youth don't last for ever. It's always as well to heed the warnings in the glass, that's what I say.

SID: Anyway, so far as June and I are concerned, I don't really see any harm in waiting a little longer.

MRS PIMBLE [*ramming home*]: Lord, no, Mr Lovejoy! June hasn't even got her trousseau yet. Take me at least five or six weeks to make that.

MRS FLOWER [*coming in from the direction of the bedrooms*]: June says her ears are burning and she's going to get up and see what's happening. She's just having a tidy-up in the mirror and putting on a new face.

MRS PIMBLE: It's been the turn of Mr Lovejoy and me for a nice little chat, hasn't it, Mr Lovejoy? [*Risking it*] Going to marry our June he is, as soon as I've had time to fix her up with a trousseau.

MRS FLOWER [*as* SID *reacts violently*]: Ooooh, Mr Lovejoy, you naughty boy! Just wait till I tell Grandpa. He'll be bouncing about that cellar like a two-year-old. [*At the kitchen door*] Look at him, Hetty! He's blushing!

MRS PIMBLE [*as* MRS FLOWER *goes into the kitchen*]: Careful how you go down them cellar-steps, Grandma! We don't want you ending up in a nasty mess at the bottom. [*To* SID] You have to be very careful where you put your feet when you go down there. Them steps can be very treacherous.

SID [*mechanically*]: So I've been hearing.

D

MRS PIMBLE: Oh?

SID: Mrs Flower was telling me about someone who used to be a parachutist.

MRS PIMBLE: I thought as much. I told her not to go scaring you with stories about Leslie Moon. That's all over and done with now, so we don't talk about it any more.

SID: Mrs Flower said he used to be June's young man.

MRS PIMBLE That's right. Lovely big man he was, standing six-foot-four in his stockinged feet. First time June brings him home he has to go head-over-heels down the cellar-steps. Broke his neck in two, clean as a whistle. Poor old Grandpa very nearly had a heart-attack on the spot. Well, you can imagine what it must be like to have a six-foot-four paratrooper come down on top of you, dead as a door-knocker.

[SID _reacts violently and almost bounces out of his chair. There is a rumbling sound as a train passes overhead. All the glass cases rattle against the wall_]

SID [_slowly getting up_]: I think I'll have a little walk in the yard, if you don't mind. Perhaps I'll just go and look at the rabbit.

MRS PIMBLE: What's the matter, Mr Lovejoy? You look all hot and bothered.

SID: I'll be all right, Mrs Pimble. I could just do with a bit of fresh air, that's all.

MRS PIMBLE: Maybe you'd like a little lay-down too, Mr Lovejoy.

SID [_going into the kitchen_]: No, I'd rather move around, if

you don't mind. I'll just go and have a look at ... er ... ·
what was her name?

MRS PIMBLE: At June's little Delia. [*Following him into the
kitchen*] Yes, well, while you're doing that, I'll make a
cup of tea. The times that kettle's been on and off the boil
this afternoon is nobody's business.

[MR PIMBLE *and* JUNE *come in from the direction of the
bedrooms*]

JUNE: Where's my Sid gone?

MRS PIMBLE [*off, from the kitchen*]: Is that you, June?

JUNE: Yes, Mum. Where's my Sid?

MRS PIMBLE [*off, from the kitchen*]: He's just gone to have a
peep at Delia. Settle yourself nice and comfortable love.
[*Coming into the room*] There now! I've put the kettle on.
Are you feeling better now, June dear?

JUNE: I'm all right, Mum. Just a bit shook up, that's all.

MRS PIMBLE: Well, I don't wonder with all that's been happening. Still, Mr Lovejoy and me have been talking things
over and I don't think it'll be long now before you'll find
yourself all nicely buttoned up, love.

JUNE [*seeing* SAMMY'S *bowl on the table*]: Oh, Mum! I wish
you'd taken Sammy's bowl away 'stead of it sitting up
there on the table like a watery grave.

MRS PIMBLE: Oh dear! Grandma could have done that little
job for me with all the bother I've been having. [*Calling*]
Grandma! Where are you?

MRS FLOWER [*off*]: In the kitchen, dearie.

MRS PIMBLE [*as* MRS FLOWER *comes in*]: Well, couldn't you have got rid of Sammy's bowl for me 'stead of standing out there looking as if you'd just got the message. What's the matter with you?

MRS FLOWER: I was just wondering why Mr Lovejoy was having a little lay-down in the yard.

MRS PIMBLE: What do you mean, 'having a little lay-down in the yard'?

MRS FLOWER: I don't know, dear. First of all I thought he was sunbathing. But I think he must be drunk.

JUNE: What do you mean, Grandma? Sid hasn't never been drunk in his life. He's teetotal.

MRS FLOWER: Well, all I know is he's having a little lay-down in the yard. Looked funny to me. I just stood in the kitchen doorway and laughed.

MRS PIMBLE [*off, from the yard*]: Jack! Come and help me with Mr Lovejoy. He's fainted.

MR PIMBLE [*hurrying off*]: Oh, Christmas!

JUNE: What on earth has he wanted to do a silly thing like that for?

MRS PIMBLE [*off*]: You go back in, June, and make sure the sofa's clear. Come along now, Jack! Get hold of his feet!

JUNE [*as they carry* SID *in*]: Is he going to be all right, Mum? He looks just like Grandma when she's had one of her nasty turns.

MRS PIMBLE: My word! I've never known anyone quite so heavy. I can't hold on much longer. [*To* MRS FLOWER *who is hovering about with the goldfish bowl still in her hands*] What are you standing about for, Grandma? Go and fetch some water.

MRS FLOWER [*proffering the bowl*]: I've got some here, dear.

MRS PIMBLE: Not that, you daft ha'porth! Haven't you any more sense than to go giving a man water what's been in a goldfish bowl? Go and get some fresh from the tap.

[MRS FLOWER *goes into the kitchen.* MR *and* MRS PIMBLE *have now got* SID *on to the settee*]

JUNE: Is he all right, Mum?

MRS PIMBLE: He doesn't look a very good colour. I don't know as we didn't ought to call the doctor.

JUNE [*shaking him*]: Come along, Sid! Perk up, love!

MRS PIMBLE: Stop shaking him, June, for Heaven's sake!

JUNE: Well, he looks so still.

MRS PIMBLE: You won't do no good by shaking.

MR PIMBLE: If you ask me, Hetty, Mr Lovejoy's going to be still for longer than we bargained for.

JUNE: What do you mean, Dad?

MR PIMBLE: Well, he ain't going to do no more moving, that's for certain.

MRS PIMBLE: Jack! You don't mean . . .?

MR PIMBLE: I'm afraid I do, love. June's Mr Lovejoy's snuffed it! He's dead.

JUNE [*in the thinnest voice imaginable*]: Dead?

MR PIMBLE: Dead as mutton.

[JUNE's *thin wail emerges out of the silence. This time there must be no mistake about it—it'll go on for days*]

MRS PIMBLE: I don't know what's wrong with this house, honest I don't. Nothing we have ever lasts five minutes. If it's not animals it's husbands. My poor June'll be driven clean out of her mind one of these days, you mark my words!

MR PIMBLE [*dazed*]: I knew Mr Lovejoy had a weak heart, but I never dreamed he'd be taken as sudden as this.

MRS PIMBLE: I thought there was something funny about him as soon as I mentioned Leslie Moon breaking his neck. He guessed—that's what I think. Went out into the backyard and died of shock. Thirty-five my June is and if he wasn't her last chance I'll eat my hat.

JUNE [*howling*]: It's Fate, that's what it is! Fate didn't like June having her Sid so she come and took him away.

MR PIMBLE: Oh, Christmas!

MRS PIMBLE: Don't carry on, June—there's a dear!

JUNE: As soon as I grab a bit of happiness it all falls to pieces in my hands.

MRS PIMBLE: Stop it, June! You're upsetting your poor mother. Why don't you be a good girl and come and have a lay-down?

JUNE [*howling even louder*]: That's what Fate's done to my Sid—sent him to have a lay-down. The long lay-down from which there isn't no getting up.

[MR PIMBLE *has a violent fit of coughing.* MRS FLOWER *reappears with the glass of water*]

MRS PIMBLE: Oh, for Heaven's sake, Jack, stop coughing and give me a hand with June.

JUNE [*shrieking*]: Sid knew what he was doing when he brought you them roses. Never wanted to cause no bother did my Sid. Even went to the trouble of bringing his own wreath.

MRS PIMBLE: Now don't you go worrying about Mr Lovejoy, June. Mum'll do for him what she did with Leslie Moon. She'll take him down to Grandpa and get him to do him up again as good as new. Before you can turn round Grandpa will have him looking all sweet and smiling in a nice glass case.

[JUNE *has hysterics. Above the din is the sound of a train rumbling overhead. All the glass cases rattle against the wall*]

THE END

A Separate Peace

TOM STOPPARD

CAST

A Separate Peace

SCENE I: *The office of the Beechwood Nursing Home. Behind the reception counter sits a uniformed nurse. It is 2.30 a.m. A car pulls up outside.* JOHN BROWN *enters. He is a biggish man in his late forties, with a well-lined face: calm, pleasant, implacable. He is wearing a nondescript suit and overcoat, and carrying two zipped grips. Looking around, he notes the neatness, the quiet, the flowers, the nice nurse, and is quietly pleased.*

BROWN: Very nice.

NURSE: Good evening . . .

BROWN: 'Evening. A lovely night. Morning.

NURSE: Yes . . . Mr . . .?

BROWN: I'm sorry to be so late.

NURSE [*shuffling papers*]: Were you expected earlier?

BROWN: No. I telephoned.

NURSE: Yes?

BROWN: Yes.

NURSE: I mean . . .?

BROWN: You have a room for Mr Brown.

NURSE [*realisation*]: Oh!—Have you brought him?

BROWN: I brought myself. Knocked up a taxi by the station.

NURSE [*puzzled*]: But surely . . .?

BROWN: I telephoned, from the station.

NURSE: You said it was an emergency.

BROWN: That's right. Do you know what time it is?

NURSE: It's half past two.

BROWN: That's right. An emergency.

NURSE [*aggrieved*]: I woke the house doctor.

BROWN: A kind thought. But it's all right. Do you want me to sign in?

NURSE: What is the nature of your emergency, Mr Brown?

BROWN: I need a place to stay.

NURSE: Are you ill?

BROWN: No.

NURSE: But this is a private hospital . . .

[BROWN *smiles for the first time*]

BROWN: The best kind. What is a hospital without privacy? It's the privacy I'm after—that and the clean linen. . . . [*A thought strikes him*] I've got money.

NURSE: . . . the Beechwood Nursing Home.

BROWN: I require nursing. I need to be nursed for a bit. Yes. Where do I sign?

NURSE: I'm sorry, but admissions have to be arranged in advance except in the case of a genuine emergency—I have no authority—

BROWN: What do you want with authority? A nice girl like you. [*Moves*] Where have you put me?

NURSE [*moves with him*]: And *you* have no authority—

BROWN [*halts*]: That's true. That's one thing I've never had. [*He looks at her flatly*] I've come a long way.

NURSE [*wary*]: Would you wait just one moment?

BROWN [*relaxes*]: Certainly. Have you got a sign-in chit? Must abide by the regulations. Should I pay in advance?

NURSE: No, that's quite all right.

BROWN: I've got it—I've got it all in here—

[*He starts trying to open one of the zipped cases, it jams and he hurts his finger. He recoils sharply and puts his finger in his mouth. The* DOCTOR *arrives, dishevelled from being roused*]

NURSE: Doctor—this is Mr Brown.

DOCTOR: Good evening. What seems to be the trouble?

BROWN: Caught my finger.

DOCTOR: May I see?

[BROWN *holds out his finger: the* DOCTOR *studies it, looks up: guardedly*]

Have you come far?

BROWN: Yes. I've been travelling all day.

[*The* DOCTOR *glances at the* NURSE]

BROWN: Not with my finger. I did that just now. Zip stuck.

DOCTOR: Oh. And what—er—

NURSE: Mr Brown says there's nothing wrong with him.

BROWN: That's right—I—

NURSE: He just wants a bed.

BROWN: A room.

DOCTOR: But this isn't a hotel.

BROWN: Exactly.

DOCTOR: Exactly what?

BROWN: I don't follow you.

DOCTOR: Perhaps I'm confused. You see, I was asleep.

BROWN: It's all right. I understand. Well, if someone would show me to my room, I shan't disturb you any further.

DOCTOR [*with a glance at the* NURSE]: I don't believe we have any rooms free at the moment.

BROWN: Oh yes, this young lady arranged it.

NURSE [*self-defence*]: He telephoned from the station. He said it was an emergency.

BROWN: I missed my connection.

DOCTOR: But you've come to the wrong place.

BROWN: No, this is the place all right. I don't want to be a nuisance.

DOCTOR: Did you try the pubs in the town?

BROWN: I'm not drunk.

DOCTOR: They have rooms.

BROWN: I've got a room. What's the matter?

DOCTOR [*pause*]: Nothing—nothing's the matter. [*He nods at the nurse*] All right.

NURSE: Yes, doctor. [*Murmurs worriedly*] I'll have to make an entry . . .

DOCTOR: Observation.

BROWN [*cheerfully*]: I'm not much to look at.

NURSE: Let me take those for you, Mr Brown. [*The cases*]

BROWN: No, no, don't you. [*Picks up cases*] There's nothing the matter with me. . . .

[BROWN *follows the* NURSE *inside. The* DOCTOR *watches them go, picks up* BROWN's *form, and reads it. Then he picks up the phone and starts to dial*]

SCENE 2: BROWN's *private ward. A pleasant room with a hospital bed and the usual furniture. One wall is almost all window and is curtained.* BROWN *and the* NURSE *enter.* BROWN *puts his cases on the bed. He likes the room.*

BROWN: That's nice. I'll like it here.

NURSE: Will you be all right?

BROWN: Oh yes, I'm all right now. Picture window.

NURSE: The bathroom is across the corridor.

BROWN [*peering through curtains*]: What's the view?

NURSE: Well, it's the drive and the gardens.

BROWN: Gardens. A front room. What could be nicer?

[NURSE *starts to open case*]

NURSE: Are your night things in here?

BROWN: Yes, I'll be very happy here.

[NURSE *opens the case, which is full of money—bank notes*]

NURSE: Oh—I'm sorry—

[BROWN *is not put out at all*]

BROWN: What time is breakfast?

NURSE: Eight o'clock.

BROWN: Lunch?

NURSE: Twelve o'clock.

BROWN: Tea?

NURSE: Three o'clock.

BROWN: Supper?

NURSE: Half past six.

BROWN: Cocoa?

NURSE: Nine.

BROWN: Matron's rounds twice a day?

NURSE: Yes.

BROWN: Temperatures?

NURSE [*turning back his bed*]: Morning and evening.

BROWN: Change of sheets?

NURSE: Monday.

BROWN: Like clockwork. Lovely.

[*The* DOCTOR *enters with* BROWN's *form and Elastoplast*]

DOCTOR: Excuse me.

BROWN: I was just saying—everything's A1.

DOCTOR: I remembered your finger.

BROWN: I'd forgotten myself. It's nothing.

DOCTOR: Well, we'll just put this on overnight.

[*He administers Elastoplast*]

BROWN: Must be wonderful to have the healing touch. I should get to bed now—you look tired.

DOCTOR: Thank you. I expect Matron will be along to discuss your case with you tomorrow.

BROWN: My finger?

DOCTOR: ... Well, I expect she'd like to meet you.

BROWN: Be pleased to meet her.

DOCTOR: Yes ... A final point, Mr Brown. This form you filled in ... Where it says permanent address, you've put down Beechwood Nursing Home.

BROWN: Yes. Well, you never know what the future brings, but for the while I like to think of it as home. ...

SCENE 3: *The hospital office. It is morning, and the* DOCTOR *is at the desk, telephoning.*

DOCTOR: ... I have absolutely no idea ... The nurse said it looked like several hundred pounds. ... His savings, yes. Frankly, I wouldn't be too keen on that—I don't really want the police turning up at the bedside of any patient who doesn't arrive with a life history. ... I think we'd get more out of him than you would, given a little time, and we'd certainly keep you informed ... No, he's not being difficult at all. ... You don't need to worry about that—he doesn't seem very keen to run away. He seems quite happy. ...

SCENE 4: BROWN's *private ward.* BROWN *is in striped pyjamas, eating off a tray. A second nurse*—NURSE COATES [MAGGIE]—*is waiting for him to finish so that she can take his tray away.* MAGGIE *is pretty and warm.*

BROWN: The point is not breakfast in bed, but breakfast in bed without guilt. Rich men's wives can bring it off, but if you're not a rich man's wife then you've got to be ill. Lunch in bed is more difficult, even for the rich. It's not any more expensive, but the disapproval is harder to ignore. To stay in bed for tea is almost impossible in decent society, and not to get up at all would probably bring in the authorities. Even if you had the strength of character there's probably a point where it becomes certifiable. But in a hospital it's not only understood—it's expected. That's the beauty of it. I'm not saying it's a great discovery—it's obvious really: but I'd say I'd got something.

MAGGIE: If you'd got something, there wouldn't be all·this fuss.

BROWN: Is there a fuss?

[MAGGIE *doesn't answer*]

They should leave well alone. I'm paying my way. . . . Are you pretty full all the time?

MAGGIE: Not at the moment, not very.

BROWN: You'd think a place as nice as this would be very popular.

MAGGIE: Popular?

BROWN: I thought I might have to wait for a place, you know. Of course, it's a bit out the way, no passing trade, so to speak. I'm very fond of the English countryside myself.

MAGGIE: Where do you live?

BROWN: I've never lived. Only stayed.

MAGGIE: You should settle down somewhere.

BROWN: Yes, I've been promising myself this.

MAGGIE: Have you got a family?

BROWN: I expect so.

MAGGIE: Where are they?

BROWN: I lost touch.

MAGGIE: You should find them.

BROWN [*smiles*]: Their name's Brown.

[*The* MATRON *enters: she is not too old, and quite equable*]

MATRON: Good morning.

BROWN: Good morning to you. You must be matron.

MATRON: That's right.

BROWN: I must congratulate you on your hospital, it's a lovely place you run here. Everyone is so nice.

MATRON: Well, thank you, Mr Brown. I'm glad you feel at home.

[MAGGIE *takes* BROWN's *tray*]

BROWN: I never felt it there. Very good breakfast. Just what the doctor ordered. I hope he got a bit of a lie-in.

[MAGGIE *exits with the tray, closing the door*]

MATRON: Now, what's your problem, Mr Brown?

BROWN: I have no problems.

MATRON: Your complaint.

BROWN: I have no complaints either. Full marks.

MATRON: Most people who come here have something the *matter* with them.

BROWN: That must give you a lot of extra work.

MATRON: But it's what we're here for. You see, you can't really stay unless there's something wrong with you.

BROWN: I can pay.

MATRON: That's not the point.

BROWN: What is the point?

MATRON: This is a hospital. What are you after?

BROWN [*sadly*]: My approach is too straightforward. An ordinary malingerer or a genuine hypochondriac wouldn't have all this trouble. They'd be accepted on their own terms. All I get is a lot of personal questions. [*Hopefully*] Maybe I could *catch* something ... But what difference would it make to you?

MATRON: We have to keep the beds free for people who need them.

BROWN: I need this room.

MATRON: I believe you, Mr Brown—but wouldn't another room like this one do?—somewhere else? You see, we deal with physical matters—of the body—

BROWN: There's nothing wrong with my *mind*. You won't find my name on any list.

MATRON: I know.

BROWN [*teasing*]: How do you know? [*She doesn't answer*] Go for the obvious, it's worth considering. I know what I like: a nice atmosphere—good food—clean rooms—a day and night service—no demands—cheerful staff— Well, it's *worth* thirty guineas a week. I won't be any trouble.

MATRON: Have you thought of going to a nice country hotel?

BROWN: Different kettle of fish altogether. 1 want to do nothing, and have nothing expected of me. That isn't possible out there. It worries them. They want to know what you're at—staying in your room all the time—they want to know what you're *doing*. But in a hospital it is understood that you're not doing anything, because everybody's in the same boat—it's the normal thing. Being a patient. That's what I'm cut out for, I think—I've got a vocation for it.

MATRON: But there's nothing wrong with you!

BROWN: That's why I'm *here*. If there was something wrong with me I could get into any old hospital—free. As it is, I'm quite happy to pay for *not* having anything wrong with me. If I catch something, perhaps I'll transfer. I don't know, though. I like it here. It depends on how my money lasts. I wouldn't like to go to a city hospital.

MATRON: But what do you want to do here?

BROWN: Nothing.

MATRON: You'll find that very boring.

BROWN: One must expect to be bored, in hospital.

MATRON: Have you been in hospital quite a lot?

BROWN: No. I've been saving up for it. ... [*He smiles*]

SCENE 5: *The hospital office. The* DOCTOR *is phoning at a desk.*

DOCTOR: No luck? ... Oh. Well, I don't know. The only plan we've got is to bore him out of here, but he's disturbingly self-sufficient. . . . Mmm, we've had a psychiatrist over . . . Well, he seemed amused . . . Both of them, actually; they were both amused . . . No, I shouldn't do that, he won't tell you anything. And there's one of our nurses— she's getting on very well with him . . . something's bound to come out soon . . .

SCENE 6: BROWN's *ward.* BROWN *is in bed with a thermometer in his mouth.* MAGGIE *is taking his pulse. She removes the thermometer, scans it and shakes it.*

MAGGIE: I'm wasting my time here, you know.

BROWN [*disappointed*]: Normal?

MAGGIE: You'll have to do better than that if you're going to stay.

BROWN: You're breaking my heart, Maggie.

MAGGIE [*almost lovingly*]: Brownie, what are you going to do with yourself?

BROWN: Maggie, Maggie . . . Why do you want me to do something?

MAGGIE: They've all got theories about you, you know.

BROWN: Theories?

MAGGIE: Train-robber.

BROWN: That's a good one.

MAGGIE: A spy from the Ministry.

BROWN: Ho ho.

MAGGIE: Embezzler.

BROWN: Naturally.

MAGGIE: Eccentric millionaire.

BROWN: Wish I was. I'd have my own hospital, just for myself. I'd have the whole thing—with wards all named after dignitaries you've never heard of—and nurses, doctors, specialists, West Indian charladies, trolleys, rubber floors, sterilised aluminium, flowers, stretchers parked by the lifts, clean towels and fire regulations. . . . All built round me and staffed to feed me and check me and tick me off on a rota system.

MAGGIE: It's generally agreed you're on the run.

BROWN: No, I've stopped.

MAGGIE: Fixations have been mentioned.

BROWN: But you know better.

MAGGIE: I think you're just lazy.

BROWN: I knew you were the clever one.

MAGGIE [*troubled, soft*]: Tell me what's the matter, Brownie?

BROWN: I would if there was.

MAGGIE: What do you want to stay here for then?

BROWN: I like you.

MAGGIE: You didn't know I was here.

BROWN: That's true. I came for the quiet and the routine. I came for the white calm, meals on trays and quiet efficiency, time passing and bringing nothing. That seemed enough.

I never got it down to a person. But I like you—I like you very much.

MAGGIE: Well, I like you too, Brownie. But there's more in life than that.

[MATRON *enters*]

MATRON: Good morning.

BROWN: Good morning, matron.

MATRON: And how are we this morning?

BROWN: We're very well. How are you?

MATRON [*slightly taken aback*]: *I'm* all right, thank you. Well, are you enjoying life?

BROWN: Yes thank you, matron.

MATRON: What have you been doing?

BROWN: Nothing.

MATRON: And what do you want to do?

BROWN: Nothing.

MATRON: Now really, Mr Brown, this won't do, you know.

BROWN: Why not?

MATRON: You mustn't lose interest in life.

BROWN: I was never very interested in the first place.

MATRON: Wouldn't you like to get up for a while? Have a walk in the garden? There's no reason why you shouldn't.

BROWN: No, I suppose not. But I didn't come here for that. I must have walked thousands of miles, in my time.

MATRON: It's not healthy to stay in bed all day.

BROWN: Perhaps I'll *get* something.

MATRON: Well, isn't there anything you could do indoors?

BROWN: What do the other patients do?

MATRON: The other patients are here because they are not well.

BROWN: I thought patients did things ... [*vaguely*] Raffia-work ...

MATRON: Does that appeal to you?

BROWN: No.

MATRON: I suppose you wouldn't like to make paper flowers?

BROWN: What on earth for? You've got lots of real ones.

MATRON: *You* haven't got any.

BROWN: Well, no one knows I'm here.

MATRON: Then you must tell somebody.

BROWN: I don't want them to know.

MATRON: Who?

BROWN: Everybody.

MATRON: You'll soon get tired of sitting in bed.

BROWN: Then I'll sit by the window. I'm easily pleased.

MATRON: I can't let you just languish away in here. You must do *something*.

BROWN [*sighs*]: All right. What?

MATRON: We've got basket-weaving . . . ?

BROWN: Then I'll be left alone, will I?

SCENE 7: *The hospital office. The* DOCTOR *is on the phone.*

DOCTOR: Well, *I* don't know—how many John Browns *are* there in Somerset House? . . . Good grief! . . . Of course, if it's any consolation it may not be his real name . . . I know it doesn't help . . . That's an idea, yes . . . His fingerprints . . . No, no, I'll get them on a glass or something—Well, he might have been in trouble some time. . . .

SCENE 8: BROWN's *ward.* BROWN *is working on a shapeless piece of basketry.* MATRON *enters.*

MATRON: What is it?

BROWN: Basketwork.

MATRON: But what is it for?

BROWN: Therapy.

MATRON: You're making fun of me.

BROWN: It is functional on one level only. If that. *You'd* like me to make a sort of laundry basket and lower myself in it out of the window. That would be functional on *two* levels. At least. [*Regards the mess sadly*] And I'm not even blind.

Ladies and gentlemen—a failure! Now I suppose you'll start asking me questions again.

[MATRON *silently dispossesses* BROWN *of his basketry*]

MATRON: What about *painting*, Mr Brown?

[*That strikes a chord*]

BROWN: Painting . . . I used to do a bit of painting.

MATRON: Splendid. Would you do some for me?

BROWN: Paint in here?

MATRON: Nurse Coates will bring you materials.

BROWN: What colours do you like?

MATRON: I like all colours. Just paint what you fancy. Paint scenes from your own life.

BROWN: Clever! Should I paint my last place of employment?

MATRON: I'm trying to help you.

BROWN: I'm sorry. I know you are. But I don't need help. Everything's fine for me. [*Pause*] Would you like me to paint English countryside?

MATRON: Yes, that would be nice.

SCENE 9: *The hospital office. The* DOCTOR *is on the phone.*

DOCTOR: No . . . well, we haven't got anything against him really. He's not doing any *harm*. No, he pays regularly. We can't really refuse. . . . He's got lots left . . .

SCENE 10: BROWN's *ward.* BROWN *is painting English countryside all over one wall. He hasn't got very far but one sees the beginnings of a simple pastoral panorama, competent but amateurish.* MAGGIE *enters, carrying cut flowers in a vase.*

MAGGIE: Hello— [*She notices*]

BROWN: I'll need some more paint.

MAGGIE [*horrified*]: Brownie! I gave you drawing paper!

BROWN: I like space. I like the big sweep—the contours of hills all flowing—I don't paint leaves, I make you see trees in clumps of green.

MAGGIE: Matron will have a fit.

BROWN: What are the flowers?

MAGGIE: You don't deserve them.

BROWN: Who are they from?

MAGGIE: Me.

BROWN: Maggie!

MAGGIE: I didn't buy them.

BROWN: Pinched them?

MAGGIE: Picked them.

BROWN: A lovely thought. Put them over there. I should bring *you* flowers.

MAGGIE: I'm not ill.

BROWN: Nor am I. Do you like it?

MAGGIE: Very pretty.

BROWN: I'm only doing it to please matron really. I could do with a bigger brush. There's more paint, is there? I'll need a lot of blue. It's going to be summer in here.

MAGGIE: It's summer outside. Isn't that good enough for you?

[BROWN *stares out of the window: gardens, flowers, trees, hills*]

BROWN: I couldn't stay out there. You don't get the benefits.

MAGGIE [*leaving*]: I'll have to tell matron, you know.

BROWN: You don't get the looking after. And the privacy. [*He considers*] I'll have to take the curtains down.

SCENE 11: *The hospital office.*

MATRON: It's not as if he was psychotic.

DOCTOR: Or Picasso.

MATRON: What did the psychiatrist think?

DOCTOR: He likes it.

MATRON: About *him*.

DOCTOR: He likes him too.

MATRON [*sour*]: He's likeable.

DOCTOR: He knows what he's doing.

MATRON: Hiding.

DOCTOR: From what? . . . [*Thoughtfully*] I just thought I'd let him stay the night. I wanted to go back to bed and it seemed

the easiest thing to do. I thought that in the morning ...
Well, I'm not sure what I thought would happen in the
morning.

MATRON: He's not simple—he's giving nothing away. Not
even to Nurse Coates.

DOCTOR: Well, keep her at it.

MATRON: She doesn't need much keeping.

SCENE 12: BROWN's *ward.* BROWN *has painted a whole wall
and is working on a second one.* MAGGIE *sits on the bed.*

MAGGIE: That was when I started nursing, after that.

BROWN: Funny. I would have thought your childhood was
all to do with ponies and big stone-floored kitchens ...

MAGGIE: Goes to show. What was your childhood like?

BROWN: Young ... I wish I had more money.

MAGGIE: You've got a lot. You must have had a good job ...?

BROWN: Centre-forward for Arsenal.

MAGGIE: You're not fair! You don't give me anything in
return.

BROWN: This painting's for you, Maggie ... If I'd got four
times as much money, I'd take four rooms and paint one
for each season. But I've only got money for the summer.

MAGGIE: What will you do when it's gone?

BROWN [*seriously*]: I don't know. Perhaps I'll get ill and have to go to hospital. But I'll miss you, Maggie.

MAGGIE: If you had someone to look after you you wouldn't have this trouble.

BROWN: What trouble?

MAGGIE: If you had someone to cook your meals and do your laundry you'd be all right, wouldn't you?

BROWN: It's the things that go with it.

MAGGIE: You should have got married. I bet you had chances.

BROWN: Perhaps.

MAGGIE: It's not too late.

BROWN: You don't think so?

MAGGIE: You're attractive.

BROWN [*pause*]: What are you like when you're not wearing your uniform?

MAGGIE [*saucy*]: Mr Brown!

BROWN [*innocent, angry*]: I didn't mean—!

MAGGIE [*regretful*]: Oh, I'm sorry. . . .

BROWN [*calm*]: I can't think of you not being a nurse. It belongs to another world I'm not part of any more.

MAGGIE: What have you got about hospitals?

BROWN: A hospital is a very dependable place. Anything could be going on outside. Since I've been in here—there could be a war on, and for once it's got nothing to do with me. I don't even know about it. Fire, flood and misery of all kinds, across the world or over the hill, it can all go on, but this is a private ward; I'm paying for it. [*Pause*] There's one thing that's always impressed me about hospitals—they've all got their own generators. In case of power cuts. And water tanks. I mean, a hospital can carry on, set loose from the world. The meals come in on trays, on the dot—the dust never settles before it's wiped—clean laundry at the appointed time—the matron does her round and temperatures are taken; pulses too, taken in pure conditions, not affected by anything outside. You need never know anything, it doesn't touch you.

MAGGIE: That's not true, Brownie.

BROWN: I know it's not.

MAGGIE: Then you shouldn't try and make it true.

BROWN: I know I shouldn't.

[*Pause*]

MAGGIE: Is that all there is to it, then?

BROWN: You've still got theories?

MAGGIE: There's a new one. You're a retired forger.

BROWN: Ha! The money's real enough.

MAGGIE: I know.

BROWN: How do you know?

MAGGIE [*shamefaced*]: They had it checked.

[BROWN *laughs*]

BROWN: They've got to make it difficult. I've got to be a crook or a lunatic.

E

MAGGIE: Then why don't you tell them where you came from?

BROWN: They want to pass me on. But they don't know who to, or where. I'm happy here.

MAGGIE: Haven't you been happy anywhere else?

BROWN: Yes. I had a good four years of it once.

MAGGIE: In hospital?

BROWN: No, that was abroad.

MAGGIE: Where have you been?

BROWN: All over. I've been among French, Germans, Greeks, Turks, Arabs. . . .

MAGGIE: What were you doing?

BROWN: Different things in different places. [*Smiles*] I was painting in France.

MAGGIE: An artist?

BROWN: Oh very. Green and brown. I could turn a row of tanks into a leafy hedgerow. Not literally. Worse luck.

SCENE 13: *The hospital office. The* DOCTOR *is on the phone.*

DOCTOR: . . . He meant camouflage . . . Well, I realise that, but there are a number of points to narrow the field . . . His age, for one thing. I *know* they were all the same age . . . Must be records of some kind . . . Service in France and Germany, probably Cyprus, Middle East—Aden possibly . . .

SCENE 14: BROWN's *ward*. BROWN *has painted two walls and is working on a third.*

MAGGIE: It's very nice, Brownie. Perhaps you'll be famous and people will come here to see your mural.

BROWN: I wouldn't let them in.

MAGGIE: After you're dead. In a hundred years.

BROWN: Yes, they could come in then.

MAGGIE: What will you do when you've finished the room?

BROWN: Go back to bed and pick up the threads of my old life. It'll be nice in here. Hospital routine in a pastoral setting. That's kind of perfection, really.

MAGGIE: You could have put your bed in the garden.

BROWN: What's the date?

MAGGIE: The 27th.

BROWN: I've lasted well, haven't I?

MAGGIE: How old are you?

BROWN: Twice your age.

MAGGIE: Forty-four?

BROWN: And more. [*Looking close*] What are you thinking?

MAGGIE: Only thinking.

BROWN: Yes?

MAGGIE: Before I was born, you were in the war.

BROWN [*moves*]: Yes. Private Brown.

MAGGIE: Was it awful being in the war?

BROWN: I didn't like the first bit. But in the end it was very nice.

MAGGIE: What happened to you?

BROWN: I got taken prisoner.

MAGGIE: Oh. Well, you're still private, aren't you, Brownie?

BROWN: Better than being dead.

MAGGIE: Being private?

BROWN: A prisoner. . . . Four years.

MAGGIE: Is that where you were happy?

BROWN: Yes. . . . Funny thing, that camp. Up to then it was all terrible. Chaos—all the pins must have fallen off the map. The queue on the beach—dive bombers and bullets. Oh dear, yes. The camp was like breathing out for the first time in months. I couldn't believe it. It was like winning, being captured. Well, it gets different people in different ways. Some couldn't stand it and some went by the book—yes, it's a duty to escape. They were digging like ferrets. They had a hole out of my hut right into the pines. There were twenty in the hut and I watched all nineteen of them go off. They were all back in a week except one who was dead. I didn't care what they called me, I'd won. The war was still going on but I wasn't going to it any more. They gave us food, life was regulated, in a box of earth and wire and sky, and sometimes you'd hear an aeroplane miles up, but it couldn't touch you. On my second day I knew what it reminded me of.

MAGGIE: What?

BROWN: Here. It reminded me of here.

SCENE 15: *The hospital office. Present are the* DOCTOR, MATRON *and* MAGGIE. *The* DOCTOR *is holding a big book—a ledger of admissions, his finger on a line.*

DOCTOR: John Brown. And an address. [*Looks up*] It was obvious. [*To* MAGGIE] Well done.

MAGGIE [*troubled*]: But does it make any difference?

MATRON: What was he doing round here?

DOCTOR: Staying with relatives—or holiday, we can find out.

MATRON: So long ago?

DOCTOR: Compound fracture—car accident. The driver paid for him ... Well, something to go on at last!

MAGGIE: But he hasn't done anything wrong, has he?

SCENE 16: BROWN'S *ward. The painting nearly covers the walls.* BROWN *is finishing it off in one corner.*

BROWN: I was a Regular, you see, and peace didn't match up to the war I'd had. There was too much going on.

MAGGIE: So what did you do then?

BROWN: This and that. Didn't fancy a lot. I thought I'd like to be a lighthouse keeper but it didn't work out. Didn't like the company.

MAGGIE: Company?

BROWN: There were three of us.

MAGGIE: Oh.

BROWN: Then I thought I'd be a sort of monk, but they wouldn't have me because I didn't believe, didn't believe enough for their purposes. I asked them to let me stay without being a proper monk but they weren't having any of that. . . . What I need is a sort of monastery for agnostics.

MAGGIE: Like a hospital for the healthy.

BROWN: That's it.

MAGGIE [*exasperated*]: Brownie!

[*He paints*]

BROWN: Shouldn't you be working, or something?

MAGGIE: I'll go if you like.

BROWN: I like you being here. Just wondered.

MAGGIE: Wondered what?

BROWN: I'm telling you about myself, aren't I? I shouldn't put you in that position—if they find out they'll blame you for not passing it on.

MAGGIE: But you haven't done anything wrong, have you, Brownie?

BROWN: Is that what you're here for?

MAGGIE: No.

[BROWN *finishes off the painting and stands back*]

BROWN: There.

MAGGIE: It's lovely.

BROWN: Yes. Quite good. It'll be nice, to sit here inside my painting. I'll enjoy that.

SCENE 17: *The hospital office. The* DOCTOR *is on the phone.*

DOCTOR: ... Brown. John Brown—yes, he was here before, a long time ago—we've got him in the records—Mmm—and an address. We'll start checking ... there must be *somebody.* ...

SCENE 18: BROWN'*s ward. The walls are covered with paintings.* BROWN *is sitting on the bed. The door opens and a strange nurse*—NURSE JONES—*enters with* BROWN'*s lunch on a tray.*

JONES: Are you ready for lunch—? [*Sees the painting*] My, my, aren't you clever—it's better than anyone would have thought.

BROWN: Where's Maggie?

JONES: Nurse Coates? I don't know.

BROWN: But—she's my nurse.

JONES: Yours? Well, she's everybody's.

BROWN [*worried*]: You don't understand—she's looking after *me,* you see.

[*The* DOCTOR *enters;* NURSE JONES *leaves*]

DOCTOR [*cheerful*]: Well, Mr Brown—good news!

BROWN [*wary*]: Yes?

DOCTOR: You're going to have visitors.

BROWN: Visitors?

DOCTOR: Your sister Mabel and her husband. They were amazed to hear from you.

BROWN: They didn't hear from *me*.

DOCTOR: They're travelling up tomorrow. All your friends had been wondering where you'd got to—

BROWN [*getting more peevish*]: What friends?

DOCTOR: Well, there's an old army friend, isn't there—what's his name—?

BROWN: I don't know. Where's Nurse Coates gone?

DOCTOR: Nowhere. She's round about. I think she's on nights downstairs this week. I understand that you were here once before—as a child.

BROWN: Yes.

DOCTOR: You *are* a dark horse, aren't you? To tell you quite frankly, we did wonder about you—some quite romantic ideas, not entirely creditable either—

BROWN: I told you—I told you there was nothing like that—Why couldn't you—?

DOCTOR: Your brother-in-law said something about a job, thought you might be interested.

BROWN [*angrily*]: You couldn't leave well alone, could you?

DOCTOR [*pause; not phoney any more*]: It's not enough, Mr Brown. You've got to ... *connect.* ...

SCENE 19: *The hospital office.* BROWN *appears, dressed, carrying his bags, from the direction of his room. He sees* MAGGIE *and stops. She sees him.*

MAGGIE: Brownie! Where are you going?

BROWN: Back.

MAGGIE: Back where?

[*He does not answer*]

You've got nothing to run for, have you. Nothing to hide. I *know* you haven't.

BROWN: I know you know. They've been busy ... I wasn't worth the trouble, you know.

MAGGIE: You blame me.

BROWN: No. No, I don't, *really.* You had to tell them, didn't you?

MAGGIE: I'm sorry—I—

BROWN: You thought it was for the best.

MAGGIE: Yes, I did. I still do. It's not good for you, what you're doing.

BROWN: How do you know?—*you* mean it wouldn't be good for *you.* How do you know what's good for me?

MAGGIE: They're coming tomorrow. Family, friends; isn't that good?

BROWN: I could have found them, if I'd wanted. I didn't come here for that. [*Comes up to her*] They won. [*Looks out through front doors*] I feel I should breathe in before going out there.

MAGGIE: I can't let you go, Brownie.

BROWN [*gently mocking*]: Regulations?

MAGGIE: I can't.

BROWN: I'm free to come and go. I'm paying.

MAGGIE: I know—but it *is* a hospital.

BROWN [*smiles briefly*]: I'm not ill. Don't wake the doctor, he doesn't like being woken. [*Moves*] Don't be sorry—I had a good time here with you. Do you think they'll leave my painting?

MAGGIE: Brownie . . .

BROWN: Trouble is, I've always been so *well*. If I'd been *sick* I would have been all right.

[*He goes out into the night*]

THE END

Fancy Seeing You, Then

STEWART CONN

CAST

HOWATT
WAITER
MURRAY

Fancy Seeing You, Then

SCENE: *The outside courtyard of a London public house. A table with a rather dingy faded-red sun umbrella, with a drinks advertisement round the side.*

HOWATT is at the table, reading a newspaper. He tries, with the paper, to swat a fly that has been annoying him.
He returns to his paper.
The fly returns to him.
Again he swipes out at it, but misses.
The WAITER approaches, in line of fire.

HOWATT: Sorry.

WAITER: That's quite all right, sir.

HOWATT: Come off it, all that 'sir' stuff. Howatt's the name. Not remember?

WAITER [*flicking the table with his napkin, and clearing away two empty glasses*]: I'm sorry, I'm new here, sir.

HOWATT: I'll have a pint.

WAITER: Draught?

HOWATT: Red Barrel.

WAITER: Certainly, sir.

[HOWATT *opens his mouth to speak, but does not do so.*
The WAITER exits. HOWATT has another go at the fly]

HOWATT: Pint of ruddy fly-killer, more to the point. Ought to be a law against flies in pubs. All I can say.

[*He starts reading his paper again. Pause, then* MURRAY *enters.* MURRAY *catches sight of* HOWATT, *then looks away. As he is walking past,* HOWATT *looks up and sees him—then looks away—then quickly back again. He opens his mouth, hesitates, then calls*]

HOWATT: Murray?

MURRAY [*turning*]: Mm? Yes . . .?

HOWATT: Bill . . . Murray . . .?

MURRAY: Yes. That's right. Heavens above. It's you! Fancy seeing you, then.

HOWATT: I knew it was you. First glance. At least, I was pretty sure. Stone the crows, fancy seeing you again, after all these years, eh! Fancy barging into you right here. What are you for?

MURRAY: I've ordered a half-pint. The waiter'll bring it out . . .

HOWATT: Make it a pint. No? Oh well . . . I wasn't positive, but I was pretty sure. I mean, you haven't changed that much. Not much at all.

MURRAY: I suppose not . . . really . . .

HOWATT: My hair's different, now. Used to be combed straight back, remember . . . used to be long, too, much longer . . .

MURRAY: That's right. I remember. And you've put on weight. Round here, haven't you?

HOWATT: Bit, maybe.

MURRAY: Yes, thank goodness you called me across. Or I wouldn't have been sure.

HOWATT: I was ninety per cent certain, myself. But you never know. Seeing you down here, I mean. Well, you can never be absolutely sure. That's why I just said your name, sort of questioning, like that. So that if it hadn't been you, you needn't have answered. Stone the crows. It's been a long time, Bill old man.

MURRAY: Yes. Yes, it has.

HOWATT: Living down here?

MURRAY: No. Down for a conference. Just staying the week-end, then back up Monday.

HOWATT: What's it like?

MURRAY: The job?

HOWATT: No. Up there.

MURRAY: Same as ever. Dull. Like it always was. But I couldn't live down here. Couldn't stand the pace. And the heat, all the humidity.

HOWATT: Here we are.

[WAITER *enters with the drinks*]

MURRAY [*making to pay*]: I'll get them.

HOWATT [*preventing him*]: Not on your life . . .

MURRAY: But—

HOWATT: Money I'm making? Don't you believe it. [*He pays*] Cheers, Bill.

MURRAY: Cheers.

[*Pause*]

HOWATT: No, I haven't been back up the old place for three years. Except one Christmas. Didn't stay long. Ran into trouble with the old girl, hours I was keeping, mean to say, she didn't understand London hours. Got all niggled, me coming in three, four in the morning. Parties and that. Just a different wavelength. Best thing I could do was leave. Left her a wad, beat it. Only stayed four days. Haven't been back since.

MURRAY: Sorry about that.

HOWATT: Sorry? No need. Best thing. Send her some cash every so often. Used to, that is. Till she got herself set up again. I've never met him. Seems to be okay. Okay for her, that's the main thing. She wasn't long shacking up, mind you, after the old man popped it. Cheers again!

MURRAY: Cheers.

HOWATT: Different way of life. Like you were saying. Different world down here. The old Flower Power, bells round the necks, bare feet in the old tube, sort of style. Fancy that walking up Renfield Street on a Saturday night? Get lifted as soon as look at you, mate. No, they wouldn't understand. See, me and the bird, we set off, out for a meal Saturday evening, do a show, somewhere up west, then after that into the club for a few—then on for a bit of a flutter, the old red and black, keep that up till anything, say three or four in the morning. Like I said, a different world. How'd you expect them to understand? Another thing, the money. Don't earn my kind up beyond Scotch Corner, tell you that, mate. In with the girl's old man, in the estate business. Commission, car, the lot. Plus extras. Enough to keep me going, not that I need it.

MURRAY: I thought—

HOWATT: What? Oh, the wife? No, only lasted about six months. She got me in the cart, mate. Got me to marry her, said she was in the club. Well, after six months, I started putting two and two together. And got out, fast. All the same, them birds. Except this one just now—the boss's girl. She's a doll. Loaded, too, tell you that. How's about yourself?

MURRAY: Can't complain. Dad's retired now. . .

HOWATT: Didn't like to ask. Okay, is he?

MURRAY: Fine, thanks. They both are. Looking better than I've ever seen them. And the girls are both engaged. Sally gets married next October. Bloke from Newcastle.

HOWATT: Quite a handful, old Sal, eh? Cheers, anyway.

MURRAY: Cheers.

[*Pause*]

HOWATT: Where are you living?

MURRAY: Still Falkirk.

HOWATT: Still living in Falkirk. What a place. You don't mind it?

MURRAY: Happy enough.

HOWATT: Still living in ruddy Falkirk. I can't get over folk, at this moment, still living in Falkirk. Still, if they all came down here, I suppose it'd make the tubes more crowded than ever.

MURRAY: I suppose it would.

HOWATT: I'm in Highgate. Coming place, Highgate. Lovely part. All done up, me and the girl's uncle did it all up. Saved a fortune. Spent it all on fitting, mind you. In a mews. Never think you were in the middle of London. A balcony. Sit out in the sun, week-ends. When I'm not away.

MURRAY: You away a lot?

HOWATT: Depends. Paris, a fortnight ago.

MURRAY: Paris?

HOWATT: Shooting.

MURRAY: Rifle shooting?

HOWATT: Small bore. Competition. Won seven thousand francs.

MURRAY: Could you bring it into the country? Easily enough?

HOWATT: Not on your life. Give it all to the government? No, I've a bank account out there. Take it out any time I please. Next visit. Well set up, boy.

MURRAY: Sounds like it.

HOWATT: Oh, Jim Howatt's well set up, take that from me, mate. I know what side my cookie's buttered.

MURRAY: Say that again . . .

HOWATT: Another? [*Calls*] Waiter!

MURRAY: Let me get them this—

HOWATT: Forget it. On me.

MURRAY: But—

HOWATT: Two pints, Waiter.

MURRAY: Half-pint for me, really . . . Jim.

HOWATT: Okay, get the other half later. Pint for me, thanks.

WAITER: Pint and a half-pint, sir. Right you are.

MURRAY: Remember Heddle?

HOWATT: Who?

MURRAY: Heddle.

HOWATT: No.

MURRAY: Sat next to you in Spike's.

HOWATT: Yes, I remember him.

MURRAY: Had a squint.

HOWATT: In both eyes. What about him?

MURRAY: Nothing, really. I just thought of him, all of a sudden. You knew Spike was dead?

HOWATT: No. Is he?

MURRAY: Yes. Few months back.

HOWATT: Pity, that. Never liked him much.

MURRAY: Me neither. Bully.

HOWATT: Ruddy pervert, ask me. Cheers anyway . . .

[*This as* WAITER *returns with drinks.* HOWATT *pays again*]

HOWATT: Thanks, Waiter. Keep the change. Do you know how to make an elephant fly? No? Get a thirty-inch zip.

[*He laughs*]

WAITER: Thank you, sir. [*He takes change, exits*]

MURRAY: Cheers.

HOWATT: Sure.

[*Pause*]

MURRAY: I was trying to think when I last saw you.

HOWATT: Falkirk. Can't get over it, neither I can—folk still living in ruddy Falkirk. . .

MURRAY: Yes, but when?

HOWATT: Good bit back. Must be all of five years.

MURRAY: If not more. I must have been on leave from National Service.

HOWATT: More than five years, that. More like seven.

MURRAY: Could be. Anyway, I remember—it was coming out of the pictures, remember, the one at the corner of the High Street?

HOWATT: That's right. That's going back some, eh? Lot of water.

MURRAY: Too true. Must've been after I finished National Service, then.

HOWATT: Must have been.

MURRAY: Were you not still in?

HOWATT: I wasn't National Service.

MURRAY: Signed on, didn't you?

HOWATT: **Yes.**

MURRAY: Air Force?

HOWATT: No.

MURRAY: Thought it was.

HOWATT: I'm just out eighteen months ago.

MURRAY: Thought you only signed on for three years?

HOWATT: Twelve. Got invalided out. Eighteen months ago.

MURRAY: I was sure you were in the Air Force.

HOWATT: S.R.S.

MURRAY: What?

HOWATT: S.R.S.

MURRAY: What's that?

HOWATT: It doesn't exist.

MURRAY: What do you mean, doesn't exist?

HOWATT: Except to those that's in it.

MURRAY: What does it stand for?

HOWATT: Special Reserve Squadron.

MURRAY: Never heard of it.

HOWATT: That's what I mean.

MURRAY: And you were in it?

HOWATT: Yep.

MURRAY: Well ... where were you based?

HOWATT: All over the place. Wherever we were needed.

MURRAY: How do you mean?

HOWATT: Well, I shouldn't be talking about it. But I can give you the general picture, more or less. If you want me to.

MURRAY: Was it sort of . . . Special Branch?

HOWATT: Special commando unit. Special training. Picked men. Ready to move wherever they were needed. We were sent wherever we were requested. What I said, about being all right for capital—that's what I mean. When I got invalided out, they had to give me a lump sum. Part for that, part blood money. In lieu of pension. I took the lot.

MURRAY: Blood money?

HOWATT: Trained to kill.

MURRAY: Away!

HOWATT: They don't take married men. Don't like men with dependants at all. Means too many questions, if anything goes wrong. We're all carefully scrutinised, before we join. Then we have this training course. And after that, we form a platoon, ready to travel at a moment's notice. Do the job, then . . . finish.

MURRAY: Fighting?

HOWATT: In-fighting. Say someone wants someone mopped up, put out of the reckoning, we were the mob that got sent.

MURRAY: For instance?

HOWATT: I was in Jordan. When the palace guard got theirs.

MURRAY: What if you get caught?

HOWATT: We never get caught.

MURRAY: If you get taken prisoner?

HOWATT: Britain doesn't know anything about us. We get examined before we go out there. No tabs, identity cards, not a fag packet left on us. Government never heard of us. We're on our own. That's why the money's so good.

MURRAY: And if you get killed?

HOWATT: Accident. Knocked down by a truck, something like that. That's why they like no dependants—no-one to kick up a fuss, start an investigation, write to their MP, sort of thing.

MURRAY: What uniform do you wear?

HOWATT: All depends. Time of Suez, I was in an Israeli uniform. We moved in before it came into the open.

MURRAY: And your pay?

HOWATT: Pretty good. Plus blood money. It makes a difference. In our line, you have to shoot first, ask questions later. Hard luck on the few, but it's the only way. The way they'd treat you, if the tables were reversed. I was offered a commission, but I didn't want it. Stayed a Sergeant. Suited me fine. I liked it, in with the boys there. All with continental bank accounts. Nothing in our own names.

MURRAY: Fantastic.

HOWATT: Just how it was.

MURRAY: What sort of training did you have?

HOWATT: Tell you one thing, it wasn't peanuts. Six-day assault course. Away in the country. Last three days, live ammo. The real thing. Barbed wire, the lot. We had to try and seize this hill, you know, that was held by one of the staff training guys. He was in a dug-out, with all the buttons and things. And we had to take a hillside. Trenches all dug, wired and that, and real ammunition.

MURRAY: You mean he had a rifle?

HOWATT: Ruddy machine guns, all over. And grenades. With trip-wires. So that we set them off, crawling through the undergrowth. Guns all over. Up to us to keep our heads down. Out of their way.

MURRAY: Were there casualties?

HOWATT: Two deaths, on our course. That's where I got this. [*Indicates under chin*] Sixteen stitches in under there. Caught on a loose strand of barbed wire. Bloke next me got his. Set off half the hillside, down on top of him. I was the lucky one.

MURRAY: Makes you think.

HOWATT: Couldn't swallow for a month. Tubes up my nose, down my throat, all over. Lost four months' seniority over that.

MURRAY: Nearest to James Bond I've ever come across.

HOWATT: Don't you kid yourself. This was the real thing. It's what it does to you, that's what you don't think of. I mean, I was dead lucky, at the end. It was dum-dum bullets got me. In here. [*Pats his chest*] Right across. Miracle they missed the lungs. Made one hell of a mess. Real miracle. Anyway, they had to operate on me, series of operations all winter, then out to convalesce. You know, not just get the wounds better, but re-adjust to civvie street. Re-acclimatise to civilian life. If it hadn't been for that year, I don't know what'd have happened. That's the trouble with some of the boys, when they come out. All happens so sudden. One minute, in the thick of it. Then, out they come. No acclimatisation, nothing. And they can't settle. All they can do is kill. That's what I mean, they aren't so lucky. As me. Ought to be on a ruddy leash . . .

MURRAY: You mean . . .

HOWATT: Look, mate. Me, with a knife. At twelve feet. Deadly. Just like that.

MURRAY: Judo?

HOWATT: And karate. Give exhibitions. Me and a couple of the pals. Black belt stuff. Tour the halls. Over to the old Continent every so often. Displays and that. I still do training every week-end, keep my hand in. It's all mind over body.

MURRAY: Reckon you'd find Falkirk a bit dull, right enough . . .

HOWATT: Falkirk'll never see me for smoke. The Big Smoke, eh? Cheers. Time you had another. I'll be back in a minute.

MURRAY: Pint?

HOWATT: Half-pint. Puts the weight on, too much mid-week. I'll get them.

[HOWATT *rises, takes glasses, exits.* MURRAY *gazes at the table, then lifts the newspaper, glances through it halfheartedly. He starts to whistle, softly to himself*]

MURRAY [*to himself*]: Howatt ... Jim ... Howatt ... [*He shakes his head*].

[*The* WAITER *enters, with two half-pints. He puts them on the table*]

WAITER: Friend of yours then?

MURRAY: What about him?

WAITER: Nothing. Just wondered.

MURRAY: What?

WAITER: Live down here?

MURRAY: Who, him?

WAITER: No, you.

MURRAY: No.

WAITER: Thought not. Scotch?

MURRAY: Scots.

WAITER: Glasgow?

MURRAY: No. Falkirk.

WAITER: Where's that then?

MURRAY: North of Glasgow. North-east.

WAITER: Mmm.

MURRAY: Half way to Edinburgh. Among the bings. You know ...

WAITER: Your friend from Falkirk too?

MURRAY: Yes. Yes, he is. Originally. Seems he's a regular here.

WAITER: Wouldn't know. I'm new myself.

MURRAY: I see.

MURRAY [*taking out money*]: How much am I due you?

WAITER: Paid for already. [*He nods towards* HOWATT, *who has just entered*]

HOWATT [*sitting*]: Ta.

[WAITER *exits*]

Looks like rain.

MURRAY: Wouldn't be surprised. [*Pause*] Your mother know ... what you were in?

HOWATT: No. No-one knows. But for you. Wouldn't like you to go saying anything.

MURRAY: Not me. Never see her nowadays, anyway. Not likely to. Since I've moved.

HOWATT: Cheers!

MURRAY: Cheers!

[*They drink*]

HOWATT [*after a pause*]: Can't get over seeing you, down here. Just like that. When are you down next?

MURRAY: Couldn't say, for sure. Maybe a couple of months. Depends when the next meeting is. Next conference.

HOWATT: Sure. I'm usually in here, lunch-time. Fridays and Wednesdays, anyway. Sometimes evenings, week-ends, with the girl. Pity there wasn't longer this time. When do you go back up?

MURRAY: Back up Monday.

HOWATT: Fly?

MURRAY: Train. Sleeper. Don't take to flying.

HOWATT: It's the only way.

MURRAY: I don't take to it. Not really. Never feel happy. See the fares are going up again.

HOWATT: Never stop.

MURRAY: That's true.

[*They drink*]

This re-acclimatisation. It must be hell. To get used to it.

HOWATT: Controlling your reactions. That's the main difficulty. Your reflexes. See that waiter? If he was to drop something, say, behind me, I'd be round in a flash. Couldn't stop myself. Not so bad now. But I was at one party, me and the girl, not long after I got my release. And someone dropped a glass, right at my back. There I was, round in a flash, and at him. Made a proper damn fool of myself. Oh, I talked my way out of it, made a joke of it. But I was lucky. Could have been serious. That's the sort of thing that stays with you. Years of intensive training, you can't ditch it all, just like that. Sheer reflex. The girl, she keeps an eye on me.

MURRAY: Is there nothing can be done? You'd think they'd have some sense of responsibility . . . towards you . . .

HOWATT: Not much they can do. Up to yourself. Oh, they keep tabs on you. Tabs on every man that comes out. Follow you around, tail you, for a long time. I got used to it. Seeing the same guy shadowing you, getting in and out the tube. Funny sort of a feeling. For your own good, mind you. They have to watch your contacts, never mind anything else. I suppose they'd put the chop on you, soon as look at you, if they thought you were up to anything. I'm one of the lucky ones, mind you. I look after two of my boys, you know.

MURRAY: Look after?

HOWATT: Couple that got invalided out. Wheelchairs ever since. Military hospital. I'm all they've got. No relations, anything of that sort. I visit them, oh, every third week-end. Take them out. Short spell. Should see them, too. Pleased as punch, every time. Soon as they see me at the doorway, at the head of the ward, their backs straighten up. Coming to attention. Drilled to it. Bloody sad, so it is. One of the penalties. Like I say I'm one of the lucky ones.

[*Pause*]

MURRAY [*looks at watch*]: Well . . .

HOWATT: The old enemy?

MURRAY: The old enemy. Know how it is.

HOWATT: Sure. When you go back up? Monday?

MURRAY: That's right.

HOWATT: Pity. Could have had a night on the batter. You and me and the girl. How about Sunday, then? I could maybe—

MURRAY: No. Sunday's out, I'm afraid.

HOWATT: What, fixed up?

MURRAY: No, it's the end of the conference, and we all have to—

HOWATT: Why not skip it? I'll see you fixed up all right. No trouble at all. Guarantee you a good night. Take in a show, like I said. Then move on. West. Have a ball. Maybe it's not such a good idea. Anyway, you're tied up. Some other time.

MURRAY: Sure.

HOWATT: When you say you were down again?

MURRAY: October.

HOWATT: Month of October.

MURRAY: I'll look in here. If I'm down, last week in October. I'll look in, on the off-chance of seeing you. For a quick drink.

HOWATT: Wednesday or a Friday's best.

MURRAY: Just on spec. Always a chance.

HOWATT: You ever go to the Palais on a Saturday night these days?

MURRAY: Haven't been for years.

HOWATT: It'll be a different class of people go nowadays, I suppose. Different category altogether. See the team's not doing so well.

MURRAY: Say that again. They've had their troubles. No gate. No gate worth speaking of. No support.

HOWATT: That's the way it goes. These wee provincial teams, all the same. All on the way out. Same in every walk of life. Big time or nothing. That's the way it goes.

MURRAY: I'll give your love to Falkirk, anyway.

HOWATT: It could do with somebody's love.

[*Pause*]

MURRAY: And next time, the drinks are on me. [*He rises*]

HOWATT [*also rising*]: What way do you go?

MURRAY: Nearest tube.

HOWATT: On the corner. Bakerloo. That do you?

MURRAY: Fine. What about you?

HOWATT: I'll hang on a bit. Sweat it out, know how it is!

MURRAY: Well, great to see you, bang into you again. Like that. After so long.

HOWATT: Sure. Glad the old man's well enough. Always had a liking for him.

MURRAY: You never know—we might see one another pretty soon again. Just the way things go, isn't it! Thanks for the drink.

HOWATT: Sure.

MURRAY: Cheerio, then . . . Jim.

HOWATT: Cheers.

[MURRAY *exits.* HOWATT *lights a cigarette, and flicks the spent match after* MURRAY, *with his thumb. He takes up the paper, starts reading. The* WAITER *enters.* HOWATT *does not notice him. The* WAITER, *as he comes behind* HOWATT, *stumbles so that a glass crashes.* HOWATT *spins and rises from his chair in a flash. They are face to face for a moment*]

WAITER: All right, all right . . .

HOWATT: I was . . . thinking of going inside.

WAITER: Certainly, Mr . . .

HOWATT: Howatt.

WAITER: It looks like rain.

HOWATT: So it does. Have one yourself.

[HOWATT *drops a ten-shilling note on the* WAITER'*s tray*]

WAITER: Thank you very much, Mr Howatt, sir . . . I'll be with you in a moment.

[HOWATT *exits. The* WAITER *clears the table, glances up and then folds the sun-umbrella. With his napkin, he flicks the table clean. He exits*]

THE END